D1585197

Hard Labour

331.881691   SIRS, B.   Hard labour

                AS 5/86   9.95

0 283 99241 7

Hertfordshire
COUNTY COUNCIL
Community Information

2 1 MAR 2000

3/06

2 6 OCT 2007

4\12

L32a

Please renew/return this item by the last date shown.

So that your telephone call is charged at local rate,
please call the numbers as set out below:

	From Area codes 01923 or 0208:	From the rest of Herts:
Renewals:	01923 471373	01438 737373
Enquiries:	01923 471333	01438 737333
Minicom:	01923 471599	01438 737599

L32b

HARD LABOUR

BILL SIRS

SIDGWICK & JACKSON
LONDON

First published in Great Britain in 1985
by Sidgwick and Jackson Limited

Copyright © 1985 by Bill Sirs

ISBN 0–283–99241–7

Phototypeset by Falcon Graphic Art Ltd
Wallington, Surrey
Printed in Great Britain by
Biddles Limited, Guildford, Surrey
for Sidgwick and Jackson Limited
1 Tavistock Chambers, Bloomsbury Way
London WC1A 2SG

Contents

Preface

When my mother got me jobs as a newspaper delivery boy and also as a butcher's boy I never questioned things. To me it was something that had to be done – our family depended on the extra shillings – and the implications for my education and to being lead towards a lifetime of physical labour did not occur to me.

I clearly remember during the winter of 1931 when I was about eleven years old going to the butcher's after the morning at school. I was asked to take the butcher's barrow, which was a big wooden high-wheeled cart, and push it for about two miles to old Hartlepool. I had been doing this for some months, and in fine weather there was no great problem although it was certainly heavy. On this occasion however there was snow on the ground, and the barrow, it seemed, became progressively heavier as I was nearing my destination. I got within about half a mile of the shop where I was due to deliver the barrow and by that time I was almost in tears, desperately trying to push the heavily loaded barrow through the snow. For some reason I did not cry out for help but tried to struggle on hoping to complete the job without assistance. Just as I was almost at the point of not being able to go any further a workman who was on his way home from the shipyards and was walking along with two of his friends noticed my plight. He put his hand to the barrow and helped me to push it. I was tremendously relieved and most grateful for this assistance. To this day I have never forgotten the face of the man or the occasion. I think of that day as the starting-off point of hard labour in my life.

Introduction

As soon as I heard in June 1983 that Ian MacGregor, chairman of Britain's state-owned British Steel Corporation, was being moved from steel to coal to preside over the fortunes of the National Coal Board, I knew the country was in for trouble. For facing this shrewd, tough, seemingly heartless American businessman who had always hated trade unions in the USA because they dared to question his authority would be the equally dogmatic, scheming and bull-headed president of the National Union of Mineworkers, Arthur Scargill. It would be, I reflected, the battle of Goliath versus Godzilla. The ordinary people of Great Britain, especially the mining communities, would be the losers in the great fight that I was sure would ensue.

As general secretary of Britain's main steel union, the Iron and Steel Trades Confederation, I had come to know both men well. Within days of Ian MacGregor taking up his appointment as chairman of BSC – appointed to that position by Prime Minister Margaret Thatcher to run steel at a profit no matter what the cost, no matter what the consequences – I was having supper with him in the private upstairs room of a Knightsbridge chop house along with Dr David Grieves, the canny personnel chief of British Steel, and one of my colleagues. The four of us had met to discuss a motion we were shortly to speak against at the Oxford Union – the undergraduates' debating forum at Oxford University. The motion declared that the British steel industry had no future. Ian MacGregor and I shared the task of persuading the audience otherwise. In the event we won the day.

But the real purpose of that chop house rendezvous was to enable us to size each other up. The government had given him a tough remit: to bring BSC back to profitability. How much could he rely on the workforce to co-operate? Or would he have to use coercion? How fast would he move? How hard would he push us?

We needed to sound him out. We wanted the industry to be profitable too, but could we persuade him that there were ways to achieve this other than works closure and enforced redundancies? How hard would he fight for a restructuring of energy tariffs to put British industrial energy costs on a par with those of our rivals in Europe? Was this 'elderly American import' – to quote the Bishop of Durham's later description – a man who would do things in his way or a man who would act as the obedient lapdog of his generous Whitehall masters? To what extent was his mind open and receptive to other views? Would he welcome a genuine dialogue? Could he be trusted?

As we worked our way through dinner, Ian MacGregor showed every sign that he would listen, that he would work with us. And, best of all, he assured me that he would re-examine the closure of the Consett steelworks in County Durham.

Under the former chairman, Sir Charles Villiers, British Steel had announced the death sentence of the plant despite the extreme deprivation and hardship that that one single act would bring about in the community. We had fought hard and long to save the plant, but had failed to dissuade BSC's management from its act of wanton folly. Now here was the new chairman, Ian MacGregor, promising that he would order a thorough investigation. Yes, he could see the harmful social consequences of closure. Yes, he was sure that the Consett workforce was good, a unique pocket of British skill. Yes, he saw that orders on the Consett books might not move obediently to other BSC plants, but might well go abroad with the result that Britain would lose out.

But immediately after that first meeting I heard nothing. I pressed for some decision, some announcement, a stay of execution. Nothing. Then, when Ian MacGregor was finally cornered at our first formal meeting, be blurted out the truth: he had not taken any action; he could see no reason to re-examine the decision; he could not interfere with the executive actions of his predecessor.

So this was the man we were going to have to deal with. So much for co-operation, participation, dialogue or persuasion. He was obviously going to press on with single-minded determination, blinkered, obsessed, deaf to rational pleas or reasoned argument. Works were to be shut; men and women thrown on the streets.

It soon became obvious that Ian MacGregor intended to follow the tired old path: closures, redundancies, failure to turn the industry round – further closures, more redundancies and further failure. There were other ways to achieve what he and the government wanted but he was not prepared to listen.

He failed in his objective: he never did make BSC profitable. And he failed in his attempt to take the axe to the core of our business. We stopped him. It is a source of great joy to me today that my own union's skilful use of political and public relations initiatives robbed Ian MacGregor of his greatest desire – to see one, if not two, of our five big integrated plants shut down. How we did it is an exciting story which I relate in a later chapter.

But for now, suffice it to say that the real Ian MacGregor became known to me within a few weeks of our initial chop house meeting. I had hoped to meet a man who, whatever his reputation, would prove open-minded, receptive, true to his word. My disappointment was immense.

I had got to know Arthur Scargill well too. His predecessor at the National Union of Mineworkers was Joe Gormley, a sincere, practical man who had served his members and his industry well. He and I could work together; we shared the same, some would say old-fashioned, principles of public life: that you say what you mean, mean what you say, and deal with people on the basis of honour and trust.

It was not surprising then that, during the thirteen-week national steel strike into which the steel unions were forced on 2 January 1980, Joe Gormley was a tower of strength. As leader of what was a long and very difficult strike (although, as it turned out, a highly successful one), I appreciated what little help Joe and his miners were able to give.

But, up in Yorkshire, Arthur Scargill was giving us problems. Our strike was over pay: we had been offered not a single penny; we were demanding a rise 'in line with inflation'. We had deliberately avoided putting a figure to our claim: we had to preserve some flexibility (something Arthur found hard to understand). Any fool can start a strike – you have to know how you are going to end it too. That's what a lot of people forget.

Our call for an increase in line with inflation was undermined by Arthur Scargill almost from the start. He put his own figure on *our* demand. Twenty per cent – that was what the steelworkers were supposed to be after. He urged the cry at meeting after meeting and eventually many of our own steelworkers took it up. Twenty per cent!

In the event, we won 15·95 per cent – a colossal achievement. But as it was less than Arthur's magical – and mythical – 20 per cent, in the eyes of some workers, and parts of the media, we had failed.

That damaging intervention by Arthur Scargill was utterly irresponsible. But it was the way he operated: beef up the demands, excite disciples to new expectations, and then, when failure comes, make a scapegoat of those who had to wrestle with the impossible.

I tried to reason with him, but it was like talking to Ian MacGregor. So when the Goliath-versus-Godzilla battle loomed I knew what to expect. And I knew that the steel industry, the National Coal Board's biggest customer, would again be in the thick of it all. That was why the last of my ten years as general secretary of the ISTC proved to be so tumultuous.

I knew, when I became general secretary, that I had a difficult time ahead, but I did not realize just how tough it would be. I took up the post on 7 February 1975. I had been a crane driver in Hartlepool, then an ISTC full-time official, then a senior organizer, then a divisional officer, then assistant general secretary. But none of that had prepared me for what was about to hit me . . . my ten years' hard labour.

First there was the Finniston Crisis when the then chairman of British Steel, Sir Monty Finniston, announced huge redundancies and I had to call in Industry Minister Tony Benn and work with him to limit the damage Sir Monty would have wrought within the industry.

Then there was the noisy, often bitter, referendum campaign in 1975 when, almost alone among trade union leaders, I worked with Harold Wilson, Ted Heath and others to persuade Britain that we ought to stay in the European Economic Community. During those days I had an early baptism of political hellfire when I saw for the first time the tactics of the far left, who stop at nothing to win their way.

Then came the national steel strike, the longest national industrial dispute since the 1930s, superseded only by the miners' own dispute. The steel strike, although successful, drained me physically but uplifted me morally and spiritually. Threatened with imprisonment, cheered one minute and booed the next – it was a traumatic time.

Next came the spate of steel plant closures the Corporation tried to force upon us: pleading with workers to ignore the enormous redundancy payments being offered to them and dealing with their inevitable yet understandable acceptance of those golden handouts. There was also the intense parliamentary lobbying to persuade MPs and civil servants to support the domestic steel industry.

Then came the turmoil within the Labour Party that I love: the determination of the hard left to destroy it; the shock decision of those I respected to leave it; the venture I and other trade union leaders embarked upon – to turn back the Militant tide. There were our meetings at St Ermin's Hotel, London, our battles at the Party Conference, our words of warning at Wembley. And there was the ultimate joy of seeing Labour's National Executive Committee being reshaped, reformed and set on the path back to sanity.

Ten years' hard labour. During those ten years I fought for what I believed to be best for the country, best for my industry, best for the Labour Party, best for the trade union movement. I was driven by one overriding principle: that if anything lasting was to be achieved, I had to take public opinion with me. That is why I spent so much time and energy explaining to my members, to other trade unionists and to ordinary Labour Party members, in fact to all who would listen, what I was seeking to do. The media were important – I quickly learned that during the steel strike – and I sought to use them in a way few other union leaders would, or perhaps could.

Ten years' hard labour. And the last year – 1984 – was the toughest of all. And for that reason that is where I must start.

1

Miners' Strike – Steel's Dilemma

My last year, 1984, as general secretary of the Iron and Steel Trades Confederation, was to be the year when I would continue to build bridges of co-operation and understanding within the industry and gradually hand over my work and responsibilities to whoever was appointed in February to take over from me at the end of the year. Certainly, it began very well. I had struck up a good working relationship with the new chairman of British Steel, Robert Haslam, who had been brought in from Tate and Lyle and was committed to steel's success. We had managed to keep the ISTC's annual pay negotiations at the national level (despite the Corporation's determination to abandon national negotiations and settle for works-by-works local deals). And I enjoyed the experience of being made a Freeman of the City of London, an honour I greatly appreciated. But then, as I feared, came the March clash between Mr MacGregor and the miners led by Arthur Scargill.

Since taking over from Joe Gormley, Arthur had twice tried to persuade his members to take strike action – once in 1982 and once in 1983 – and both times he had lost the ballot. When Mr MacGregor announced the closure of Cortonwood and four other pits he knew there would be a furious reaction, but he must have considered that either a ballot would fail again or, if the miners did go on strike, he would beat them. I am told that he believed a ballot would fail, but he reckoned without Arthur's use of the domino effect: the Yorkshire area, as it legitimately could, declared a strike to protect its pits, and the other areas of the NUM followed the Yorkshire miners' lead. Two thirds of the miners stopped work, either because they believed it the right thing to do or because they were picketed out. The Nottinghamshire miners, however, always strongly independent in thought and deed, overwhelmingly declared that they would not strike without a national ballot.

Commentators have said that if only the NUM leadership had held a national ballot they would have had a mandate for a national stoppage, no coal would have been moved and the strike would have been more effective, shorter and successful. I am not so sure. A national ballot might have resulted in a third rejection of strike action by the NUM's membership. It is very difficult to persuade men and women to take industrial action to preserve a plant. Those workers directly affected will take action, of course. But they will only maintain that action, and it will only lead to success, if it is widespread and effective. The fact is, however, that people in one works hesitate before putting their own jobs on the line for their colleagues elsewhere. It is a sad fact of life. Those who argue that this would not be the case if there were 'the right kind of leadership' are out of touch with reality. I have held works meetings where we urged, begged, pleaded with the workforce to stand firm – or stand shoulder to shoulder with their brothers and sisters in difficulties elsewhere. While you are there, there will be cheers, applause and speeches of support. Once you have left, the plant votes to go back, cave in or call off their supportive action. It's human nature.

So Arthur Scargill, if he really believed that the way to keep open the threatened pits was to use industrial action (a view I cannot share: the NUM would have been more successful in shaping public opinion if its members had not gone on strike), was, from his standpoint, absolutely right in encouraging the domino technique. It worked – more or less. But it served to create a lot of problems, not least for those of us in the steel industry.

As I had predicted, the steel industry was very quickly at the centre of the miners' strike. As coal's second biggest customer, all attention was focused upon us. The miners would naturally be tempted to shut us down, although during our own strike there had been no attempt to close down the mining industry – a major consumer of steel. Yet any closure of steel plant, we knew, could result in the permanent closure of some works – Ravenscraig in Scotland, Llanwern in South Wales and Scunthorpe in South Humberside were at risk – with the consequent loss of up to 40,000 jobs.

Steelworkers faced a very difficult dilemma. We wanted to give all the support we could to the miners because they were absolutely right; their case was unassailable. It made no sense to shut pits because they were deemed to be 'uneconomic' when, with the rising dollar or the falling pound, a sudden increase in the price of oil could make every pit producing coal 'economic' overnight. Nor did it make sense to abandon Britain's coal assets, which future generations may well desperately need. It made no sense to put miners out of work and destroy mining communities without looking at the resultant financial and social costs. I have seen works being closed to save, say, a quarter of a million pounds a year, yet the subsequent cost to the nation is a million pounds a year in redundancy payoffs, lost income tax and national insurance contributions, and unemployment and social security payments. Too often the government looks at the profit and loss account of an individual plant or enterprise without considering the overall balance sheet of Great Britain Limited.

Yet while our sympathies were with the miners and their case, how could we agree to the threatened shut-down of our industry? Steel had experienced many difficult years. All our works were fighting for survival. Unlike other nationalized industries, steel has to compete for orders with the rest of the world. If our prices are not right or if we are thought to be unreliable, we lose orders. Exports dry up and, worse, British manufacturers go abroad for their steel. At the same time, we wanted to do what we could to help.

Of the three steelworks most at risk, Ravenscraig plant took all the coal produced at the nearby Scottish pit, Polkemmet, and supplemented this with large quantities of foreign coal imported through Ravenscraig's Hunterston coastal terminal. When Polkemmet came out on strike, coal continued to flow only through Hunterston, and steel production had to be cut by 30 per cent. At Llanwern, where coal stocks were considerable, it was some time before any problem arose. But the works relied on local indigenous coal so it was obvious that something had to be done if the furnaces were to be kept alive. At Scunthorpe there was a similar situation. The works took a substantial amount of coking coal from seven mines in the Yorkshire coalfields, and as there were no large stocks it was not long before steel production sank below 30 per cent.

Our local officials in each of these three areas therefore went into negotiations with area officials of the NUM in Scotland, Yorkshire and South Wales. Their task: to reach a local agreement which would both help the miners' cause yet protect the steel industry, and in particular enable our furnaces to maintain a good operational level. Once a furnace is starved of fuel and 'goes down' it takes months – and millions of pounds – to repair. And when you only have two or three blast furnaces available, the failure of a furnace can be the deathknell for a plant. At all three plants – Ravenscraig, Llanwern and Scunthorpe – local agreements were eventually made and both miners and steelworkers were happy. But the agreements were soon to come under pressure from coalfield militants – especially the hard left and members of the Communist Party – and from Arthur Scargill himself.

In Scotland, while we were seeking to come to an agreement with the NUM we heard that the British Steel Corporation had begun trucking coal in by road. Coal supplies from Polkemmet had ceased and supplies from Hunterston, brought by rail, were becoming spasmodic. Immediately we contacted British Steel and demanded that the trucking cease. Although we shared the Corporation's fear that a lack of coal would force the failure of a furnace, we were determined to let nothing get in the way of winning an acceptable agreement with the NUM. Our words were heeded; the lorries stopped. We expected the NUM to be delighted, but later that day we were staggered to hear one NUM official say that he personally would not rest until Ravenscraig had been forced to stop production.

If only he had realized what he was saying! For years British Steel and the government had indicated their desire to close down one of the big integrated strip mills, and only recently the ISTC had beaten Ian MacGregor's plan to shut Ravenscraig, his chosen sacrifice. Now here was an official of the NUM saying he wanted to do what Ian MacGregor had failed to do. Those of my colleagues who heard him knew that if they let the NUM shut Ravenscraig it would never open again.

Still we struggled for a local agreement, and a few days later we took a delegation of miners and railwaymen to the works to show them how low our coal stocks had become. But what they saw and what they heard failed to impress them. Within a few days the miners had persuaded local officials of the National Union of Railwaymen and the Associated Society of Locomotive Engineers and Firemen to cease all movement of coal from Hunterston. The railwaymen were joining with the militant miners to shut the plant, yet when we tackled individual railmen about what they were doing they simply shrugged their shoulders and sighed, 'It's orders from London.'

Among steelworkers, and the wider community, all hell was let loose. The Scottish TUC and the Scottish Labour Party also became alarmed as it dawned on them that the outcome of the rail union's unthinkable action would be a fatal blow to the economic heart of Scotland. Rail general secretaries Ray Buckton of ASLEF and Jimmy Knapp of the NUR, safe in their London headquarters, might be prepared to wipe out what was left of Scotland's heavy industry, but the mass of ordinary Scottish workers was not prepared to allow that to happen. So Mick McGahey, vice-president of the NUM, was pressed to visit Ravenscraig himself. Mick, although a prominent Communist, was always a practical and understanding man and realized that something had to be done. It was three days, however – on 13 April – before he was able to carry his colleagues with him and it was announced that two trainloads of coal would be delivered to the steel plant every day. In our view this was not enough, but we were prepared to live with it.

Two weeks later, however, those two trainloads a day became one. I have never discovered who was to blame for this deplorable decision – no one I spoke to would accept responsibility and Mick McGahey himself was unavailable. The British Steel Corporation, which had held back while the ISTC, acting for all steelworkers, sought to win an agreement with the miners and railworkers, decided that enough was enough and, without a word to us, went ahead and once again hired lorries to shift the coal.

On 11 May there was a bitter and stormy meeting between ourselves, the miners and the rail unions and once more an agreement was hammered out: there would be fourteen trainloads of coal delivered each week – some 18,000 tonnes – enough to safeguard the furnaces and protect regular orders, but not enough to maintain full production. Our members met the management at Ravenscraig, assured them that this time the agreement would stick, the lorries were stopped and the National Union of Railmen undertook the transfer of coal from Hunterston to the steel plant.

The patience and perseverence of the Ravenscraig steelworkers during those difficult days should be applauded. They had kept the steel plant alive, yet they had accepted a cut in production and thereby aided the miners in their struggle. In short, they had achieved what they set out to achieve. Or had they?

In Llanwern, our officials had sought from the South Wales NUM a similar agreement. On 6 April the NUM agreed that regular consignments of coal should be delivered to the plant from Nantgarw by rail. On 4 May, after long discussions, it was agreed that coal could be moved to Llanwern from the nearby Port Talbot coke works by rail, but the agreement had to be ratified a few days later at the

Welsh TUC. In the event, it was decided to have further discussion and, on 11 May, NUM observers visited Llanwern where they were shown the desperate shortage Llanwern's coke ovens and blast furnace faced. The NUM observers seemed to be convinced and my steel colleagues were sure we were inching our way to a South Wales agreement which would protect the steel industry in the area.

Sure enough, we got an agreement. Coke would be moved by rail from the Port Talbot coke ovens to Llanwern from 21 May. We were overjoyed – for a while.

2

Fighting for Scunthorpe: The Battle of Orgreave

Ravenscraig, Llanwern. What of Scunthorpe? We held a number of meetings with the Yorkshire Area NUM and quite often representatives of ASLEF and the NUR were present. Sometimes officials of the National Union of Shipping and the Transport and General Workers Union joined us. Eventually, on 9 April, our officials came to an agreement with the Yorkshire Area president, Jack Taylor, and his NUM Executive Committee colleagues. There would be a guaranteed 15,700 tonnes of coal a week for Scunthorpe. The agreement was ratified by the two rail unions, the NUS and the TGWU.

The following day Jack Taylor and his vice-president, together with officials of the rail unions and representatives of the ISTC led by my divisional officer, Roy Bishop, met the management and senior representatives of British Steel, the National Coal Board and British Rail. The supply of 15,700 tonnes of coal a week was agreed by all parties subject to the following conditions:

(a) All coal should come from one of the Yorkshire coalfields with a small amount from the Cortonwood pit (where the miners' strike started).

(b) All coal must be moved by rail.

(c) Coal and coke must not be imported through Scunthorpe's nearby Flixborough wharf.

The agreement was welcomed by the whole of Yorkshire and Humberside, but our troubles were not over. Instead of the agreed 15,700 tonnes a week coming into the plant, deliveries were often short. Not once did Scunthorpe receive more than 11,000 tonnes. We protested, but to no avail.

Then, on 21 May, Roy Bishop was contacted by Mike Lahive, the personnel director at the Scunthorpe works, who informed him that the Queen Mary blast furnace on the plant was in a precarious state. The shortfall in deliveries had taken its toll and the Queen Mary had developed problems. Unless 5000 tonnes of good metallurgical coke could be delivered to the works right away, the furnace might be severely damaged. Roy Bishop got in touch with Jack Taylor to ask whether the 5000 tonnes could be delivered on a one-off basis.

'We'll put the request to our committee in the morning,' Roy was told. Roy Bishop immediately sent a letter to Owen Briscoe, general secretary of the Yorkshire Area N U M. This is what it said:

As you are aware, we did make an agreement whereby your organisation gave dispensation for 15,700 tonnes of coal to be delivered to the above works from the Yorkshire Area pits.

Resulting from this agreement we have been able to maintain the coke ovens in a reasonable state, although there has been, in fact, less than 25% of output from the Blast Furnaces. This has led to 25% of that workforce being laid off since the 6th April and the balance of the workforce have on average been suffering a loss of earnings of 33%. Unfortunately, there has now been a development that is causing concern, not only to the management, but also to the members of both my own organisation and the National Union of Blastfurnacemen.

This development is that the dust catchers in the two remaining blast furnaces have become blocked. This blockage has been created because of an insufficient gas blow through the furnaces.

Both furnaces are now chilled and are going cold because of an insufficient supply of coke, and in the early hours of this morning there was a Burden Slip.*

---

* A dangerous collapse of many tonnes of iron ore and coke.

This has, therefore, now created a very dangerous situation for those people employed on the blast furnaces, as both furnaces have now become unstable. This afternoon, the 'Queen Mary' is to be inspected to attempt to determine what damage has been caused, but it has now become very apparent that if both furnaces are to be saved from permanent and irreparable damage there is a need for a continuous hot blow with good quality coke for 4/5 days per week for the next few weeks.

To this end, therefore, we need to request of your goodselves as a matter or urgency a variation in our present agreement in order that we receive an additional 5,000 tonnes of coke from the BSC's Orgreave Coke Ovens.

I would be obliged if you could place this letter before your Dispensation Committee at its meeting to be held on Tuesday, the 22nd May, and it would be my intention to be present in your office at approximately 11.00 a.m. in order to discuss the contents of this letter further should your Committee so decide.

I would hope that your Committee would look upon this request with favour bearing in mind that the present situation is creating a position where not only are the employees in some physical danger within the blast furnaces area but that the blast furnaces are now in serious danger of irreparable harm.

The following day, after numerous phone calls between the ISTC's divisional office and Owen Briscoe, Peter Heathfield (the NUM general secretary) and Sam Thompson (the Yorkshire Area vice-president), we were told that any variation in our agreement to permit the delivery of the 5000 tonnes of good metallurgical coke could be made only with the authorization of the Yorkshire Area Committee *and* Arthur Scargill. So now Arthur himself was becoming involved – and out hearts sank.

Roy Evans, my assistant general secretary (and subsequently my successor as general secretary of the ISTC) spoke to Neil Kinnock, Leader of the Labour Party, and Stan Orme, Labour's energy spokesman. 'You've got to understand the seriousness of the situation,' he told them. 'And you've got to get Arthur Scargill to understand.'

Danny Ward, Scunthorpe's managing director, was anxious for BSC to take unilaterial action, but we dissuaded him. 'Give us just a little more time,' we pleaded. He agreed.

I sent a copy of Roy Bishop's letter to Arthur Scargill, who was at the National Coal Board offices in London. The letter was sent by hand and marked top priority. I don't know if he even read our letter. We certainly heard nothing from him.

Meanwhile, the Queen Mary was deteriorating. There had been a further burden slip and the furnace was becoming dangerously unstable. BSC could wait no longer. Not only was the furnace facing collapse, the lives of ordinary steelworkers were now at risk. On 24 May, three days after we were first informed of the Queen Mary's plight, lorries were ordered to collect the coke from the nearby Orgreave coking plant.

As soon as the first shipment left Orgreave the NUM terminated the agreement it had with us. British Steel, sensing that the unions had fallen out among themselves, decided not to risk any more furnaces. Coke would continue to come from Orgreave and coal would be imported not through Flixborough but through other wharves on the River Trent.

The NUM did what it could to stop coke production at Orgreave. It was at Orgreave that the nation witnessed, on television, some of the biggest mass picketing and worst violence of the entire miners' dispute. It was at Orgreave that Arthur Scargill himself fell or was felled by a policeman's riot shield. Yet none of what happened at Orgreave would have taken place if BSC had given us a little more time or if the NUM in Yorkshire had had the ability to react to new situations.

In a very real sense Arthur Scargill was the author of the Orgreave chapter of errors. He accused me and my union for the Orgreave coke production. According to him, we were making the coke, we were driving the lorries, we were using the coke on the plant. Not for the first time he had got his facts wrong. Those who made the coke were members of the Transport and General Workers Union (who were, incidentally, urged by Moss Evans's headquarters in London to carry on working), the drivers were also mostly TGWU members, and those handling the coke at the works were members of the National Union of Blastfurnacemen.

At this stage, Arthur was repeatedly ranting on about the help he had given to us in our strike. Miners, he said, had lost time and money through our strike. I am afraid that this simply is not true. Miners used over 75,000 tonnes of steel during the steel strike, at a time when we were trying to stop all movement of steel. Steel was transferred from colliery to colliery to beat the steel strike, and the amount of coal the miners produced during our thirteen week stoppage was the highest for many years. During those thirteen weeks miners took home record earnings too. And when, in Wales, miners were asked to vote on whether they should support us with direct action, they voted against by five to one! So much for solidarity. Yet not once did we call the miners 'scabs'.

The worst news that came from Scunthorpe was that the Queen Mary blast furnace had suffered partial collapse. The shipment of those 5000 tonnes of coke had come too late. The other blast furnaces also suffered damage, and there was a costly stoppage for repairs and rebuilding.

The bad news from Scunthorpe was matched by bad news from Ravenscraig and Llanwern. In South Wales, before the agreement to allow rail shipments of coke from Port Talbot to Llanwern could come into force, a delegation of Llanwern steelworkers was asked to come to the headquarters of the South Wales NUM. After being kept waiting from 8.45 a.m. to 12.45 p.m. they were handed a statement which declared that all deliveries of coal and coke for Llanwern would cease on the night of Tuesday, 19 June, unless I and other steel union officials met the NUM's National Coordinating Committee to agree at national level tonnages of coke and coal to be received. And, worse, the statement went on: 'If attempts are made by the British Steel Corporation to transport coal and coke by road to the steelworks, then the NUM will request ASLEF and the NUR to stop deliveries of iron ore to all steelworks.' So, they were aiming to stop not only coke and coal but our basic raw material – iron ore.

In Scotland it was a similar story. On 29 May national officials of the NUM in Scotland announced that the Ravenscraig supply agreement, guaranteeing 18,000 tonnes of coal a week, was suspended pending national negotiations, which had to take place by 19 June. All train deliveries of coal were to cease. BSC reacted in the only way it could – by calling out the lorries again.

It was clear what had happened: Arthur Scargill, with or without the knowledge of his Executive, had forced the local area executives to pull out unilaterally of the agreements we had so carefully and so painfully made with them and demand one national agreement to be hammered out at a national summit.

I had already attended a meeting of the NUM's national coordinating committee, so I did not hold out much hope of persuading them to see the peril the steel industry was in. Indeed, at that meeting, attended by representatives of the rail unions, the NUS and the TGWU, I had explained the dilemma we faced. BSC and the government had long wanted to shut one of our integrated plants. Were they now going to aid and abet them? The answer came from the Transport Workers' Alec Kitson. Closure of one of the big five? He shrugged. 'There will have to be casualties.'

Casualties! Did he not mean fatalities? What would the people of South Wales, Scotland and Humberside say if they knew this man, and most of those in that meeting, were prepared to make unemployed more workers and destroy more communities than Ian MacGregor had ever dreamed of?

Two days before the next meeting of the National Coordinating Committee – the one mentioned in the Llanwern and Ravenscraig ultimatums – I received a personal letter from Mr Scargill. It was scurrilous, full of inaccuracies, but is worth reproducing because it gives an insight into the man.

Throughout this dispute you have displayed an attitude which can only be described as deplorable and one which is in violation of every basic principle accepted by the Trade Union and Labour Movement.

The NUM (Yorkshire Area) reached an agreement with your Union and the British Steel Corporation to supply a certain amount of fuel into Scunthorpe – an arrangement which worked for nearly 11 weeks.

The British Steel Corporation unilaterally decided to break this agreement and began transporting coke from Orgreave to Scunthorpe.

I would remind you that this coke was only produced as a result of the NUM agreeing that coal would be supplied to Orgreave in order that the ovens could be kept intact and workers not thrown out of work.

I find it disgusting that your Union now accept the use of *blackleg labour* to breach NUM picket lines and take in coke which will be used to try and defeat my members currently engaged in industrial action.

I would remind you that when steelworkers took action in 1980, my Union rigorously respected picket lines and refused to allow any steel to go into our pits or depots. I find it sickening that you are a party to this tactic, bearing in mind that miners are fighting for the right to work for the preservation of mining communities.

We have had over 2,000 members arrested, nearly 700 injured (some of them very badly), 1 man killed and several of our members in prison under the new Tory legislation.

The fact that you have acquiesced to the use of scab labour is something which will be on your conscience for the rest of your life, at a time when we are fighting to save our industry. I can only say that you are a disgrace to the very concept of the Triple Alliance and all that it was supposed to do.

The 7 June meeting, which was attended by my assistant general secretary Roy Evans and ISTC national officer Sandy Feather, was a disaster. The transport unions agreed to blockade *all* movements of coal, coke, oil and other fuels both to steel plants and to power stations until the ISTC agreed with the NUM the amount of coke and coal to be used at each of Britain's steelworks. The amount at each works was to be enough to 'keep furnaces intact and the industry safe' but not sufficient to allow for *any* production. In other words, the NUM's Coordinating Committee wanted to see the complete cessation of steel production in the UK.

Roy Evans and Sandy Feather left the meeting without comment, anxious to discuss the matter with me and the ISTC Executive, which would be meeting during our annual conference which was about to take place in Scarborough.

When I got to Scarborough I found the conference venue crawling with representatives of the media. Cameras and cables, microphones and transmission vehicles, photographers and reporters lined the route from our hotel to the meeting hall. Arthur Scargill had made a statement giving the steel unions just a few days – until 19 June (the same date as given in the Llanwern and Ravenscraig ultimatums) to agree with the NUM leadership the quota of coal for each works based on zero production. What did I have to say? I said we refused to be intimidated. We would do what was best for our industry and best for the miners – we would keep the steel industry going; if the industry collapsed, so would the sixteen British pits which fed the steel plants.

We invited one of a delegation of miners who were attending the conference to speak. He spoke well, passionately, and received a standing ovation. Later he and his colleagues told us it was madness for steelworkers and miners to be at loggerheads when the real enemy was Ian MacGregor, whom we both knew and under whom we had both suffered. They said too that they understood the dilemma we were in. The collapse of steel would not help the mineworkers one bit.

'For God's sake tell Arthur what you've told us. We're sure he'll understand.'

Our conference was determined to do what it could for the miners and naturally we took collections for the NUM to add to the £20,000 we had already given.

We decided to go into private session, excluding the

media, something I have never done before, but we did not want the world to listen in to what would be a heart-searching session in which one union would be discussing how to deal with another. The press were disappointed, but I know they understood.

Our conference could not understand why the NUM president had given his ultimatum through the press. We had received no communication from him at all. It was an extremely strange way to behave.

There were urgent pleas by delegates who feared what a cessation of production would do to their own localities. Others stressed that if a deal could be done at national level with the NUM based upon a percentage cut in steel production, then every effort ought to be made to find the right wording.

Eventually, the conference unanimously passed a resolution. It read:

> Given the deteriorating situation in the Coal Industry and the effect this is having on the supply of fuel for the Steel Industry and the additional effect on community relations in South Yorkshire, South Wales and Scotland between miner and steelworker, this Conference pledges support to the NUM in their fight to secure jobs and the safe future of their industry.
>
> However, in pledging its support this Conference calls upon the Executive Council to seek urgent meetings with the NUM Executive in order to reach agreement for satisfactory fuel supplies to the Steel Works.
>
> This Conference also calls upon the NUM to recognise the precarious state of the British Steel Industry and in particular the effect on the mining community should any works suffer irreparable harm either of a mechanical or a commercial nature resulting from inadequate fuel supplies.

It is important to remember that this resolution and the ISTC's stance were supported by every shade of political opinion within the union – right, left and centre. Supporters of Militant, the Communist Party, the Bennites, the hard left, the soft left, the mainstream Labour Party, the traditional right, all agreed on one thing: there must be no stoppage of steel production, no closure of steel plants. And there would be no bowing to threats.

The nineteenth of June passed. On 20 June I finally received a message from Peter Heathfield officially telling us that all local agreements were indeed suspended and the NUM wanted a national agreement. We responded immediately. Of course the ISTC's Executive would meet the full Executive of the NUM. If a national agreement was thought best, we would do all we could to reach one.

Ah, said Arthur Scargill the following day to the media, the national agreement would have to be based on zero steel production. When, months later, he himself protested about the National Coal Board setting preconditions on talks, I had to allow myself a smile.

3

Face to Face:
Fourteen Unions Line Up

The meeting between the full executives of the ISTC and the NUM took place on 29 June at Congress House. My Executive had decided to play it cool. They had been angered both by Arthur Scargill's letter and by the remarks he had been making about steelworkers, but they wanted to reach an agreement if at all possible. There would be no recriminations, no emotional responses to lies and intimidation. We wanted to approach what was a very important meeting in a sane and sensible manner. But if NUM officials persisted with further vindictive statements, then the ISTC Executive would respond in kind.

In the event, the meeting took place in a very restrained atmosphere. Mr Scargill cited the 1974 report 'Plan for Coal', quoted Ian MacGregor, repeated his assertion that the NCB really wanted to close seventy pits with the loss of 70,000 jobs and detailed NCB mismanagement at Polmaise colliery and at Cortonwood. We had already heard all the points he made over and over again on radio and television. He went on to say that the NUM considered it had a right to ask the ISTC for support and that we should identify with the miners' struggle. He then repeated some of the statements he had been making about the support steelworkers had received from miners during our own dispute. How his memory had dimmed!

At last Arthur came to the point. The NUM leadership wished to make an agreement which would allow for the transport of coal and coke into steel plants providing there was no production of steel. If such an agreement could not be reached, then pickets would be put on every steel plant in the land and the NUM would ask 'for observation of the basic trade union principle of not crossing picket lines.'

Once again Arthur had got it wrong. The object of picketing was originally to prevent unorganized workers going into a factory to do the work of those on strike. Nothing more. It was never a 'trade union principle' that one group of workers could picket a plant to stop another group of workers going in to do their *own* work. It was understandable when such picket lines were set up; indeed, we had pickets on steel users' gates when we were trying to persuade drivers not to move steel around the country. But that was based upon a desire to persuade and not on the belief that it was a 'trade union principle'.

And how easily that 'principle' was forgotten by Arthur and his own miners at the end of the miners' strike when pickets from Kent tried to stop Yorkshire miners going back until their sacked Kent colleagues had been taken back by the NCB. What did the Yorkshire miners do the first day? They turned back. And the second day? They walked on through the pickets. So much for the 'principle'.

What Arthur Scargill was threatening to do also contravened TUC practice. Congress states that if a trade union wishes to picket an industry not involved in an industrial dispute, this can only be done after consultation with, and with the agreement of, the unions in that industry. Not once did the NUM approach us about this.

But what shook us most was that Arthur *seemed* to be saying that unless we would agree to a total cessation of steel production, then no deal that day was possible. He had demanded this before. But here we were, in Congress House, the full executives of our two unions, with the world's media outside, seeking to *negotiate* an agreement that would allow all of us to concentrate our attack on the government's foolish, even evil, policies. Was the president of the NUM really saying to us 'Take it or leave it'?

I responded at some length, outlining the difficulties and damage that would ensue if total production ceased. We were an industry without a captive market. There could be no guarantee that at the end of the miners' strike we would be able to persuade our customers to come back so that we could resume work. And what of the Triple Alliance – the grouping of coal, rail and steel unions set up by myself, Arthur's predecessor Joe Gormley and Jimmy Knapp's predecessor Sid Weighell? That body had not even been approached by the NUM. Why this ultimatum now? Why not discussion by the bigger grouping?

I knew that many of my ISTC colleagues with me were prepared to take a cut in steel production if we could agree one – and we would all have discussed that. But a total stoppage? No way.

I looked around the table at the NUM Executive flanking their president on either side. Emlyn Williams, the much respected leader of the Welsh miners, did not have anything to say. I knew that he had already received a respectful and responsible letter from the Llanwern Trade Union Committee detailing the seriousness of the Llanwern situation. Coke ovens, the committee had pointed out, were operating below accepted safety levels. No. 1 coke oven battery had collapsed and No. 2 battery was in danger. Batteries 3, 4 and 5 were producing badly. Losing these coke ovens would mean they would not be rebuilt and much less coal would be required from local Gwent pits in the future. I looked at Emlyn Williams again. Surely those points had got home to him? Surely he was concerned about the fact the Llanwern uses 27,000 tonnes of indigenous coal a week – 25,000 tonnes of which comes from six pits in the Gwent coalfield, employing 6000 miners and thousands of ancillary workers. But Emlyn did not speak.

I looked at Mick McGahey, but again I was disappointed. I knew Mick and Arthur frequently disagreed about NUM tactics; would Mick not try to do a deal with us? But no, he criticized the amount of coal now being transported into Ravenscraig by lorry, completely ignoring the fact that that situation had only arisen because the NUM itself had reneged on our local agreement there.

Mr Scargill's last contribution was to criticize the ISTC

for allowing its members to drive the coal lorries which were by now scurrying around Britain in their thousands. I sighed. Not one ISTC member drove a vehicle during the whole of the miners' dispute. Most drivers were undoubtedly members of the TGWU. Not that I would criticize that union, it was difficult for them to control their driver members, as we had discovered during our own steel strike. But Arthur seemed to believe that the TGWU, like the rail unions, was working solidly with the NUM. He must have been living in fantasy land. The fact was that more coal was moved during the miners' dispute by lorry, and by ship, than ever before. And the rail unions had very little success in persuading the majority of their members to stop carrying coal for steel plants or power stations.

'Arthur, I must tell you, that a total steel production stoppage is unacceptable. It's not on.' I was emphatic.

The local agreements at Ravenscraig, Llanwern and Scunthorpe had worked well for a number of weeks. Could they not be resurrected? There was no reply.

Look, I said, if we could not reach agreement, then BSC would simply go ahead and do its own thing, using every means of transportation it could to move in as much coal as it wanted. Our local agreements had cut steel production. Unless they could be revived, all the coal BSC needed would be brought in and production would increase sharply. Again there was no reply.

Would the NUM executive, even at this late stage, not move from its position of zero steel production? No, it would not.

I said I would have to report the situation to all fourteen unions in the TUC Steel Committee and the meeting broke up. Although the ISTC organized over half Britain's steelworkers, the rest are members of a number of very big and important trade unions including the Amalgamated Union of Engineering Workers, the National Union of General and Municipal Workers, the TGWU and the EEPTU (Electrical Engineering and Plumbing Trade Union). They would naturally be concerned. And that is what we told the press afterwards: we were reporting the situation to the Steel Committee. It did not take them long, however, to discover that the NUM was holding to their zero production demand and that we had rejected it. But would the other thirteen unions we were about to speak to?

When we met some days later, the reaction of some of the other unions to the miners' demand was ferocious. How dare the miners demand that steelworkers smash their own industry! Every single one of the fourteen unions, including, I stress, the TGWU and left-wing unions like TASS (Technical, Administrative and Supervisory Section of the Amalgamated Union of Engineering Workers), rejected the miners' demand. That was very significant.

I captured the feeling of those fourteen unions when I said that I was not prepared to allow my industry to be sacrificed on someone else's altar. I was thinking especially of those left-wing leaders who, safe in their own offices away from the heat of the battle, had said with a shrug that there had to be 'casualties'. They were prepared to see us go up in flames provided they themselves were not singed.

BSC used every truck they could find to bring in coke and coal, and we could not oppose them. Steel plants had to be safeguarded. As it was a question of a total stoppage or using coal brought in through picket lines, then we had to choose the latter. That was something we understood very well. But would the forthcoming TUC Congress and Labour Party Conference?

4

The Dockers Take Action – and Lose

As a result of the decision by the NUM to pull out of all local agreements between steelworkers and mineworkers, and the decision of the NUM's Coordinating Committee to black supplies of coal, coke *and iron ore* to steel plants, the rail unions refused to run iron ore trains from the Immingham terminal on the coast to Scunthorpe. BSC's Scunthorpe management was left with no alternative but to use road vehicles to move the ore.

The terminal agreement allowed for TGWU dockers to work on both ship and shore. Material would normally be transported by rail, but lorries had been used from time to time since 1979, and the practice had developed whereby, with the agreement of the dockers, contractor road hauliers were used. However, two dockers had to attend every lorry loading.

But the dockers did not like BSC moving the iron ore by road during the miners' strike, so they objected. First they said there was no agreement for moving material by road. That was plainly rubbish. Then they wrongly said that the British Steel Corporation was in breach of the Dock Labour Scheme.

After arguments and delays, the lorries were finally loaded and they ran at an intensive rate over the weekend of 7-8 July. Then on the morning of 9 July, the local dockers held a mass meeting and by a narrow majority decided to go on strike immediately. Within a matter of hours a national dock strike was called, but it fizzled out very quickly.

A month later the dockers were again involved in an attempt to obtain a national docks stoppage to aid the miners. Although there had been a number of initial difficulties at the Hunterston terminal after it was commissioned in 1979, there had been no trouble for a long time. Now, the dockers were objecting to the berthing and unloading of the coal-carrying bulk carrier *Austia* in order to help the NUM in their strike action. Consultations took place between the TGWU Dockers Section, the BSC and the Clyde Port Authority. Both BSC and the Port Authority were convinced that the dockers simply wanted to stop BSC getting *Austia*'s much needed coal. It was a political strike aimed at hitting BSC (which was not involved in the coal dispute) and, ultimately, at closing down the Ravenscraig steelworks. Statements by the NUM's Scottish officials confirmed that this was the case.

BSC, after eighteen days of indecision during which the *Austia* was left anchored off the port, became alarmed at the low stocks of coal at the steel plant. So they decided to berth the boat without the use of tugs (but with the assistance of foy boatmen, whose responsibility it is to moor the vessel, belonging to a private company which operated on the Clyde with the TGWU's blessing) and to unload the coal using steelworkers who were employed at the terminal.

The dockers walked out. Again, the strike spread, but although a number of docks joined in, many of the major ports stayed out of the conflict.

At no time did any of the parties involved contact the ISTC. We were aware of what was happening, but thought it strange that the warring factions did not consult us.

Dockers in a number of ports began to realize that being involved in the dispute in no way helped their own trading prospects, so the strike was rejected dock by dock, area by area. By 14 September, seven days after the end of the TUC Congress in Brighton, it became clear that the dockers' industrial action in support of the NUM was fading. What was needed was an intervention that would enable the TGWU to make an agreement that would allow an orderly return to work.

The intervention came from Dr Jeremy Bray MP, who organized a meeting between ISTC officials at Ravenscraig and TGWU officers and shop stewards. An agreement was reached: 22,500 tonnes of coal a week would be unloaded at Hunterston and delivered to Ravenscraig. This was a much higher figure than the 18,000 tonnes limit we had agreed with the mineworkers earlier in the year, an agreement which the NUM had unilaterally broken.

The Scots miners' deputy president, George Bolton, tried to pretend that no deal had been struck, but the TGWU and the ISTC soon demolished his fantasy.

For the steelworkers, the new agreement was a good one, giving Ravenscraig that little extra assurance of life *after* the miners' strike. And, as a result of the NUM's about-face on local agreements, the collapse of the dockers' strike and the reluctance of the transport unions to endanger the steel industry, BSC tonnages went up considerably. For the dockers, the agreement enabled them to return to work. As Brian Redhead said on BBC Radio's 'Today' programme: 'It did get the dockers off the hook.' But by their refusal to move iron ore the rail unions, however, have injured their members' livelihoods in a very real way. BSC has now realized that it can transport huge quantities of coal, coke and iron ore by road. Much of these bulk materials may never return to rail. The rail unions have appealed to the TUC to ask what it can do to persuade British Steel to move back to rail. It is a bit late in the day, but in my view there are good sound economic reasons why there should be a return to rail use, and I have been adding my voice to those calling for action.

5

Crisis in Congress
– the TUC Charade

Arthur Scargill's objective was to keep the strike alive until at least after the TUC Congress in September and the Labour Party Conference in October. There was a threat of disruption of the TUC Congress at Brighton by elements in the NUM and the TUC general secretary, Len Murray, who was not in the best of health, was clearly apprehensive about the situation.

On the evening of 30 August a TUC group comprising Ray Buckton of ASLEF, David Basnett of the General and Municipal Workers, Len Murray, his deputy Norman Willis and two other TUC officals met Arthur Scargill, Mick McGahey and Peter Heathfield. The NUM president again began lecturing the group on the 1974 'Plan for Coal' (had he never heard of economic winds of change?) and went on to say that the NUM expected all trade unions to observe picket lines and not to accept 'scab' coal. A draft statement was prepared and considered.

After some variation to the suggested wording General Council members Ray Buckton and David Basnett said they would be unable to commend such a statement to the General Council without an assurance from the NUM representatives on two things. First, that the NUM's motion (already on the agenda of the TUC conference), would be put to conference unamended. Other unions like the NUR and ASLEF had tabled amendments to the NUM resolution, amongst other things demanding a levy on all trade unionists, which the TUC would have found embarrassing. These amendments would have to be withdrawn. Secondly that any lobbying of Congress by the miners would have to be orderly and peaceful. These assurances were given.

So, in order to have a peaceful conference, Len Murray and his colleagues had bought off the miners by accepting that the NUM motion would be put in its entirety without amendment and that the agreed statement would be made.

On the morning of Friday, 31 August, the General Council met in the Metropole Hotel, Brighton, and received a report of the meeting from their general secretary. When I read the statement that had been agreed the night before I could hardly believe my eyes. It read:

The General Council condemns the NCB's efforts abetted by the Government to run down the coal industry and affirms total support for the following:

(i) support for the National Union of Mineworkers' objectives of saving pits, jobs and mining communities;

(ii) a concerted campaign to raise money to alleviate hardship in the coalfields and to maintain the union financially;

(iii) To make the dispute more effective by:

(a) not moving coal or coke, or oil substituted for coal or coke, across NUM official picket lines, or using such materials taken across NUM official picket lines;

(b) not using oil which is substituted for coal.

The NUM acknowledges that the practical implementation of these points will need detailed discussions with the General Council and agreement with unions who would be directly concerned.

The General Council calls for a fresh commitment of all to an expanding coal industry.

The General Council calls on the NCB to resume negotiations immediately with the NUM to resolve this damaging and costly dispute in line with the 'Plan for Coal'.

This meant that if there was an official NUM picket line across a steel plant – or any other plant come to that – no coal or coke or substitute oil could be taken through that picket line, and that no one should use any material that came through. True, there was the qualifying passage about the NUM *acknowledging* that the practical implementation of these points would need 'detailed discussions' and 'agreement with unions who would be directly concerned'. But I knew that, so far as the NUM's leadership was concerned, this was meaningless. Indeed, within twenty-four hours of the statement being put to Congress, NUM spokesmen were saying just that.

Before the General Council began its discussion of the statement we had a short break. I went up to a couple of colleagues from the AUEW (a union that has a lot of members in steel).

'What do you think of the statement?' I asked.

'Well, we'll go along with it.'

'But surely you can't vote for it. For a start, it's not possible to operate,' I protested.

'Oh, we may as well vote for it. It won't work in any case.'

When the matter was opened for discussion it was obvious that not only the left-led unions would support the statement. Many moderate unions were also prepared to go along with it. There was a great deal of concern about the threatened disruption of Congress. If the General Council turned the statement down, all hell might be let loose. This concern was fed by stories in the national press about what might happen and which trade union officers (including myself) might be beaten up. It was a truly disgraceful state of affairs.

Len Murray tried to calm things by restating Congress practice that one union could not place a picket line at a works that was not involved in the strike unless there had been consultation and agreement with those unions directly concerned. The fact that the NUM was already doing this without any consultation at all was conveniently ignored by the unions anxious for peace.

The only two industries which would be hit by the proposed TUC statement were steel and power. So it was that Eric Hammond of the EEPTU, John Lyons of the Engineers and Managers Association (the power industry) and I for steel objected strongly and vociferously to the proposals.

I warned the General Council about the possible effect on Ravenscraig and Llanwern and said my members were not prepared to accept the collapse and closure of blast furnaces and coke ovens which would lead to the permanent closure of plant.

'Oh, they'll open up again afterwards,' I was told by Mick McGahey, who was on the General Council.

'Who will give me a guarantee that these works will reopen if closed?' I challenged him and Len Murray. There were no takers.

'And who will guarantee that our customers will come back to us after we have turned away their orders?' I persisted. Again there were no takers.

As the discussion progressed, I became more and more disheartened. It became abundantly obvious that the fate of steel was secondary in the thoughts of so many of my General Council colleagues. What they wanted above all was to buy off the miners with a set of words which did not apply to *them*. Of course the printworkers and the firemen and the postmen and all the rest could support the statement. They weren't in the firing line.

I raised the question of the picketing that was already going on without permission and against Congress principles – picketing preventing the movement of iron ore and fuel oil into major steelworks. What would the General Council do about this? Once more there was no comment.

'The rail unions are using fuel oil as a substitute for coal. What do we say to them?' Again, no comment.

And what of industry after industry using imported steel. Once the NUM had stopped British steel plants, would the unions in these industries instruct their members not to handle imported steel? I observed shuffles and embarrassment.

I then informed the General Council that under no circumstances was it possible for me to accept the statement. In my opinion, it was totally unacceptable to the members I represented, to my industry and to members of the other steel unions, some of whom did not have representatives on the General Council.

The one man who was really listening to what I said was Fred Smithies, General Secretary of the National Association of Schoolmasters and Union of Women Teachers, and he spoke up for us. Of course an industry could not be allowed to die! But the statement was adopted and given enormous publicity. And so were the views of myself, Eric Hammond and John Lyons. So we became the targets of abuse from the miners' delegates at the conference and from the ragtag and bobtail extremist hangers-on.

My wife had joined me at Brighton on the Saturday for my own union's reception at Congress. She was extremely nervous, not without just cause. She too had read in the press of the threats to general secretaries such as myself who were not prepared to sacrifice all for Arthur Scargill's cause. She insisted that I should not go running in the morning as was my usual practice, for fear of being attacked. Some of my colleagues, according to the press, were accompanied by minders to protect them from physical violence. I did not think it right to have such protection and, anyway, I usually kept fairly fit and could probably look after myself. I was certainly capable of running away!

The pressures upon me were extreme and on the Sunday I asked Joan to return home because it was not my nature to keep out of sight and hide from people who are fiercely opposed to me. I knew that when I left the hotel on the Monday morning to walk the two hundred yards to the Brighton Centre I would be an easily recognizable target for Arthur Scargill's extreme left-wing associates. I was not prepared to sneak into the hall by the back way and decided that I would face up to the whole of the howling mob, knowing full well that I was representing the views and desires of not only my union but of everyone else who worked in the steel industry; in addition, I was receiving many messages of support from the public.

Joan refused to leave; she was still in her room in a very worried state when I left the hotel after a General Council meeting, accompanied by Bill Whatley (Shopworkers), Roy

Grantham (Association of Professional, Executive and Computer Staff) and Bryan Stanley (Post Office Engineers). Hoards of photographers and television crews began to mass around me and to a certain extent they protected me from the people who wished to get at me. The cameramen obviously wanted to capture my expression as I listened to the chorus of vicious chants of 'Scab', 'Traitor', 'Judas'. People were pushing and shoving; there was not a policeman in sight to give us help had we needed any.

Then one of the crowd leaped forward and tried to land a blow in my back. I was told that he was yanked away by someone who looked like Norman Willis – if it was Norman Willis, it was his first good deed as the new general secretary of the TUC. It was a very tense moment, but I was not prepared to do other than repeat my views in public and the views of my members, and I walked on through the chanting crowd.

My delegation was terribly sad about the pressures being put upon us, quite unjustly, by the leaders of the NUM. They asked me not to make a contribution during the debate on the statement; this was a request that I was bound to accept. My members did not wish to inflame the situation nor did we want to be seen to be in opposition to the mineworkers in their struggle.

During the debate we heard some amazing speeches from trade union leaders who promised the miners the earth. Of course, as the months went by they were unable to deliver; later many miners thanked me for at least being honest. 'You explained where you stood and you got a lot of flak,' one of them wrote. 'But the others just gave us the words. They conned us.'

When we returned to London we called a meeting of the TUC Steel Committee. The thirteen other unions had told the NUM that a stoppage of steel production was not on, but at Brighton some of those unions had voted for the TUC statement which would, if enacted, have stopped every single steel plant in the UK. 'Now,' I said, 'let us stop messing. Where do we all stand?'

Once away from Brighton, all the unions were magically

of the same mind again. They met Norman Willis to tell him that the unions in steel could not do what the miners wanted them to do. Materials brought into steel plants through picket lines – reluctantly, and because of the NUM's foolishness, by lorry – *would* be used by steelworkers of all fourteen unions. Norman listened very carefully to what we said, took note of our position, made no demands upon us and asked that we do whatever was possible.

The TUC Steel Committee then met the NUM Executive, and once again we heard Arthur reciting his set piece and demanding a total shutdown of our steelworks. We invited the mineworkers to request something other than a total stoppage – a percentage reduction in output perhaps. The ISTC president, Bill Irvine, himself from Ravenscraig and a respected left-winger, made an impassioned plea to the NUM. Steelmen were prepared to suffer, indeed they had been suffering, but they could not allow their livelihoods to be wiped out. The NUM Executive was adamant. Total closure or nothing.

Looking back, I think the saddest episode was Len Murray's capitulation to the pressure the leadership of the NUM was exerting. It was clearly understood by all of us on the General Council that the statement we were being urged by Len Murray to put to conference involved breaking the law. Yet it had only been a few weeks before that I had heard Len tell the General Council, when they were discussing the National Graphical Association's conflict with Eddie Shah, that under no circumstances could he or the TUC accept the breaking of the law. I agreed with him. I voted with him. And I believe still that in a democracy like ours the law has to be respected, whether we like the legislation or not. We can always change a law by democratic means. I know that most of the TUC's General Council agrees with me. But they did not on that crucial day in Brighton or, at least, they pretended not to.

6

The Lessons Learned

I sometimes worry that my defence of the steel industry may have been misinterpreted as opposition to the miners' struggle. Nothing could be farther from the truth. I had believed in their case from day one. I had been concerned, too, about the kind of treatment they would receive from Ian MacGregor – a man with seemingly little or no social conscience. Often he had said to me, 'My concern is with the balance sheet, not the social consequences of what we do!' Soon after Mr MacGregor was moved to coal I wrote to Arthur Scargill to let him have some insight into the new chairman of the National Coal Board. I made it clear that if Mr MacGregor was to be beaten the NUM would have to use radically different tactics. Looking back over the year-long miners' strike I can only pay tribute to the miners and their families who endured so much for so long. The tragedy is that the strike *could* have been won. I am quite sure of that.

What, then, can the trade union movement learn from the dispute? Already there have been a crop of analyses from observers, but as one who was in the thick of it – and, remember, most steelworkers live with miners in coal and steel communities – I can see six distinct lessons. First, the NUM failed to set an objective; secondly, the union ignored public opinion; thirdly, it attacked and abused fellow trade unionists; fourthly, there was lack of discipline; fifthly, the NUM allowed the way the dispute was conducted to slip from its hands; and, finally, there was too little regard for democracy and the ballot box.

What was it that the miners were after? To safeguard the

pits directly under threat? To force the NCB to halt all pit closures? To achieve the best deal they could? The NUM's objective was never clear to the mineworkers, to the mining communities, to fellow trade unions or to the Labour movement at large. Had the NUM had as its objective the creation of independent arbiters who would decide, after taking all financial and social factors into consideration, whether a pit should be closed or not, I am sure the NUM could have achieved this. The arbiters would have had the final word; the decision to shut a pit would have been theirs and theirs alone.

NACODS, the ably led coal industry's supervisors' union, was able to win something like this *after* a short, sharp episode of industrial action. The only weakness with the NACODS achievement – and it was an achievement – was that the new arbiters will merely offer an opinion, they will not actually decide the future of a pit; that power still resides with management.

Towards the end of the dispute, the NUM Executive was begging the Coal Board to give the NUM what it had conceded to the National Association of Colliery Overmen, Deputies and Shotfirers (NACODS). Yet if it had gone about things differently, the NUM *could* have had arbiters *with teeth*. Many a pit would have seen its life lengthened, and for some pits under threat there would have been a reprieve.

The second lesson we can learn from the miners' strike is this: the NUM should not have ignored public opinion. I am convinced, and our experiences in the steel industry when we stopped at least one major closure bear this out, that industrial action on its own will not win the day. Unless public opinion is behind you, it is likely you will lose. Marches, slogans, rallies and strikes are useful tools to be used sparingly and with great effect. But, today, an overwhelming necessity is to win public opinion. There was no attempt at all by the NUM to win that support. There was no explanation of their case, only half a dozen phrases repeated parrot fashion by the NUM leadership when they appeared on television. Where were the booklets, the leaflets, the full-page advertisements in the national and provincial press? Where were the posters and the hoardings? The NUM persisted in doing things the old-fashioned way. Any large-scale public relations and advertising campaign costs money – but a campaign of the size necessary to swing public opinion and secure for the NUM effective arbiters would have cost *far less* than the money the NUM spent on maintaining the strike – and all to no avail.

The third mistake the NUM made was to attack and abuse fellow trade unionists. It was truly remarkable that the president of a union engaged in one of the greatest industrial struggles of all time should spend so much time antagonizing unions and individuals he would be calling upon for assistance. There was absolutely no need to erect hostile barriers by making impossible demands. There is a lesson to be learned about solidarity and trade union brotherhood; the extremists in the movement will have to realize that although they may be able to lead their organizations into disputes, it does not necessarily follow that the movement in general will be prepared to give blind support.

The fourth lesson we can learn concerns discipline. There has to be unquestioned discipline in such massive confrontations, and the NUM leadership's inability to condemn violence from the start swung the public behind the government. Everyone could see what was going on; it was no use Mr Scargill or any of his colleagues blaming the media for selective reporting. In my own union, we had steelworkers who were attacked by miners and who had to be sent to hospital. We said nothing about it – indeed, we hushed it up – but the fact was that there were incidents which should have had the outright condemnation of the NUM Executive. Often it is difficult to control strikers who are frustrated, angry and perhaps provoked, but violence can be averted if it is condemned at the outset. During our own steel strike we had tense, difficult moments, but all my divisional officers knew that at the first sign of any violent act they had to take steps to deal with it and make sure it never happened again.

When I write of discipline, I do not only mean the discipline of the rank and file, I mean the discipline necessary within the trade union movement. When a union involved in industrial action requires the assistance of other unions, this should always be sought through the TUC. This in turn will allow the TUC to be involved in the strategy being employed. Otherwise some trade union general secretary or president might well pursue policies purely for his own vainglorious ends, and the movement, with its long history of common sense and constructive work, does not wish to be saddled with embarrassing situations like that. However, the TUC itself must act with discipline and firmness. In recent months there have been two major confrontations involving the TUC. In the first, the confrontation with the NGA, the TUC was positive and decisive. But in the second, the miners' strike, the TUC was timid and apprehensive in a way I have never seen before.

The fifth lesson is that the trade union movement should never allow control of a dispute to slip from its hands. The NUM's *refusal* to uphold the local coal supply agreements that steelworkers and miners had made around the country meant that British Steel stepped in, hired transport and took control. When union speaks to union it must be on the basis of trust and mutual support; the NUM's unilateral withdrawal from honourable agreements it had entered into with a brother trade union was perhaps the beginning of the end of the miners.

The final lesson we can learn is this: if we really want a change in the way our lives are ordered, if we really want to see a transformation in the way we as a nation conduct our affairs, then we have to bring about this change, this transformation, by the ballot box.

It gives me no joy to point to the mistakes of the miners' struggle, but we must learn from them. We are living in a new age; the old ways do not always work any more. We have to reassess the situation and act accordingly.

7

The Shaping of My Early Life

My conviction that the public has to be carried with us, that the British people do not like extremes, that moderation and reasonableness will win the day, springs, I suppose, from my own upbringing.

My birthplace was a small village called Middleton, situated between Old Hartlepool and West Hartlepool on the northeast coast. I was born on 6 January 1920. My father, Frederick, was a hand riveter in the shipyards, but he was unemployed for many years during my childhood. He died over ten years ago, but my mother, Margaret, now ninety-three is living in Hammersmith. She had a hard life, with very few luxuries, but has been a wonderful person to each member of a very large family. There were ten children in our family – six boys (Frederick, myself, Robert, John, Oliver and Alan) and four girls (Edith, Margaret, Ruby and Emily). All my brothers and sisters are alive today; two of my brothers still live in Hartlepool.

My memories of home life are of two downstairs rooms in a terraced house in Middleton. At night we had to sleep what was known as 'top and tail' – with as many as five in one bed. There were two beds in one room and one bed in the room where mother and father slept.

We were very poor in the twenties and early thirties. My father was on what was known as 'Guardians' or the Means Test and only received about 27 shillings a week to keep his large family. It used to be my job as a young boy to collect firewood and sea coal for the home fires, which could be gathered free from the beaches. I went to school at Middleton St John's and at the age of ten obtained two jobs, one with the butcher and the other working for a newspaper shop.

The newspaper job meant that I had to get up at six o'clock in the morning, go to the shop, pick up a small barrow, walk to West Hartlepool just over two miles away to collect the papers, bring them back and then deliver them. I usually finished at about 8.30 in the morning and then started school at nine.

At lunchtime I would work for the butcher and then, when school had finished, at 4.30 in the afternoon, I would resume my paper round, walking to West Hartlepool, returning to Middleton and doing the deliveries to finish at 6.30 in the evening. In those days newspapers were not of the tabloid variety but were very large with a great many pages, so each night I would be running back and forth half strangled by the weight of twelve dozen papers in a mailbag strung round my neck.

At the weekend I worked all day Saturday and Sunday morning. On Saturdays I worked for the newspaper shop, starting at 6 a.m. and finishing about 9 a.m. I would then go to the butcher's shop, sweeping out and doing odd jobs until late afternoon when I would be relieved to pick up the evening papers. In the winter this job was a little more onerous due to the fact that an additional journey had to be made later in the evening to collect the *Football Mail*.

In those days very few people had radios and the radio football results service was very poor, so naturally the special football edition which came out on a Saturday evening was very important. As soon as I received my quota of papers in the *Mail* printing office I would set off at a run back to Middleton yelling to the world at large that I was selling the *Football Mail*.

On Sunday mornings I would again start early, at approximately 6.30 a.m., first of all travelling the round trip of four miles to pick up the papers and return to the paper shop. I would then help to sort the papers into order so that I could deliver them. I would finish about 9.30 a.m. Sunday was my day of rest so far as work was concerned, with more time for pleasure than any other day of the week.

For the paper job I was paid 4s 6d per week, which was a large sum in those days, and for the butcher's job 1s 6d per week. Each of my employers also gave me an additional 3d a week for myself – not to be handed to my parents, I was told. In fact I gave them every penny I earned to help keep the family clothed and fed.

My school work, of course, suffered considerably; in the mornings I quite often nodded off to sleep. It was not until the last six months of my school life, when we moved to another area and I was no longer doing two jobs, that my schoolwork picked up and I once again did well at school.

I was very active in my youth, playing cricket and football and going swimming and also messed about in the boats in the harbour near our home. Compared with young people living in cities I was very fortunate. We always had the hard sands upon which to play our games, the sea to swim in free of charge and if we needed additional food we caught fish, lobsters, crabs, mussels and winkles – all familiar fare in the days of my youth.

Life was simple and fairly straightforward. I grew up in a period which was relatively crime-free, probably because no one had anything worth stealing, but nevertheless discipline and honesty were much more prevalent in those days.

But there were sad moments. Sometimes a young friend would take to his bed with an illness and simply die. Consumption, better known nowadays as T B, diphtheria, whooping cough and scarlet fever could all be fatal, and people accepted there was no cure and waited for the end.

The village in which I lived, between Hartlepool and West Hartlepool, was in the middle of the dockland area, and I was aware of the widespread unemployment that existed in those days. Every hour of the day, every day of the week, every week of the year, one could go to the street corner and see men just walking up and down, hour after hour, talking about everything under the sun because they had nothing else to do. They had no money, and in the twenties even radios were an expensive luxury.

Sometimes, however, in the summer there would be a little light relief. I can see in my mind's eye occasions when fifteen or twenty grown men would take to the streets, run a quarter of a mile and then, one after the other, jump fully clothed off the end of the pier into the sea. They would keep this up for about an hour, to the great delight of the children who were watching. But despite the poverty and the deprivation, there was no bitterness in the minds of those men. We did not know a Communist, we had no agitators.

Looking back it is surprising that in those days, with so much unemployment and so much poverty, the people of Hartlepool returned a Conservative MP until after the Second World War. I suppose we accepted that we had to be governed by people who were either nobility or rich industrialists. I never saw or heard our MP, Mr Howard Gritten, but he had the reputation of being a nice, quiet man. The story went that the only time he ever spoke in the House of Commons during his twenty-two years was to ask someone to close the window in order to keep out the draught! I am pleased to say that the position has changed: the people of Hartlepool now take a greater interest in the election of their MP and for the past two decades have elected a moderate Socialist.

During the years of my childhood in the twenties there used to be carnivals or galas. The men from the village would enter their ragtime jazz band in the carnival competition, playing kazoos welded to large tin trumpets. They always started off with the same tune and I only discovered its name many years later – 'The New Colonial'. If the village band had been successful they would march home late at night, heads held high, playing 'We Are the Rovers, We Won the Cup'. Today it is impossible to imagine grown men marching for miles blowing kazoos in the hope of winning a couple of shillings.

At some of our carnivals we were entertained by one or two local personalities in the 'Go As You Please' competition. One I remember most vividly was a chap we used to call the Human Hairpin. He would stand on the stage and gradually turn the top half of his body completely round so that he was looking in one direction while his feet and legs were pointing in the other. This operation took about five minutes. Unfortunately he never won a prize. Then there was an Indian Army veteran, Billy Siggers, who would get up and recite 'The March to Kandahar' – I do not recall him winning a prize either.

Unemployment, of course, was the real curse at that time. Britain was probably one of the richest countries in the world but it spent little of its wealth in trying to help the poor, particularly in the Northeast. Yet the very men who were being ignored by their country and by their government, who were being subjected to the Means Test and denied the opportunity of work training, took up the challenge in 1939 and, without hesitation, answered the call to arms.

I was deeply impressed by my grandmother's approach to life. Gran Powell always helped people. She was always willing to share what she had with others and it was always possible to go to her house and have a meal. This lesson in helping others is one I have never forgotten. While I was working as a butcher's boy and a newspaper boy I used to sleep at my Gran's otherwise my father would have had his pubic assistance money reduced by 5s 6d a week.

I left school when I was fourteen. I was hoping to get an apprenticeship, as some of my schoolfriends had done. But their fathers managed to pull strings to get them in, and my father was not in a position to do that. So, after three months of unemployment, I was only able to get a job as an errand boy. Later I worked in a timber yard carrying huge baulks of timber, even railway sleepers. Employers can no longer exploit young people as I was exploited then, earning only 9s 10d per week for doing the same work as the men in the yards. Even the men in the timber yard received only 30s for a forth-eight-hour week for similar work, while the yard's owner lived in a massive mansion overlooking the park. Trade unions have played a large part in eliminating such injustices.

I was seventeen when I went into the steel industry. My father asked a foreman in the South Durham Steel and Iron Company if he would give me a job. I started on shift work at the lowest level, in a hot, dirty, dangerous rolling mill. I quickly became accustomed to the routine and the danger, and soon learned to appreciate the comradeship of the men who worked with me in the mill. I had to open the doors of a steel furnace to allow a charger crane to insert a red-hot slab or withdraw one that was white hot to be placed on the rolling mill. This operation was nonstop, and therefore I had to stay on the job and know exactly when to open and close the doors.

It was as a teenager that I met Joan, who became my wife. She too lived in West Hartlepool and we met at the roller-skating rink. She had a quietly attractive personality and was extremely pretty. I was only twenty-one and Joan only twenty when we married, but life was less complicated in those days; young people were more able to cope with the problems of married life and fewer marriages ended in separation and divorce. After a few months we managed to obtain a rented house in Helmsley Street, West Hartlepool, and we lived there for a good number of years. It was during that time that our two children were born – Margaret in 1944 and John in 1950. I had decided early on that if I ever married I would not have such a large family as my parents had had.

During the early days of my marriage I kept myself fit by physical training. I first became keen on this activity when I was a member of the Boys Welfare Club in 1935. The club had very few facilities, but did an excellent job in the field of sport and training. One of my colleagues with whom I grew up in Middleton was Ted Gardner, who later became the British Empire flyweight boxing champion. I myself subsequently took a physical training course so that I could help teach young schoolchildren in the evenings.

It was while I was in the Boys Welfare that the club became physical training champions of the whole Northeast. I was a member of the champion team and was naturally very proud of our achievement. We also took part in sports meetings in County Durham, but my only real success was as a junior of fifteen when I won the cricket-ball-throwing championship with a throw of over ninety yards.

In 1958 I became secretary of a very large branch of BISAKTA, (British Iron Steel and Kindred Trades Association), as my union was then known, and as such was entitled to be paid for the additional work this involved. This, plus the fact that I was upgraded in my job in the steelworks, meant that my financial affairs were improving. At the same time, because of my activities in the trade union and Labour movement, my horizons were broadening beyond the environment in which I lived. And so it was, in 1959, that Joan and I decided to take the plunge and buy a house. Our decision to move from Helmsley Street was also partly prompted by the government's attitude to rented accommodation which meant that the landlords were going to have a field-day. We finally bought a house on the outskirts of Hartlepool that was then being built for £2200. Our new status as householders reflected the changing attitudes of young people of those days. Although I was ahead of most of my contemporaries in buying a house, the growing desire of ordinary working people to own their own home was becoming apparent. With the decline in the number of houses available for rent, the great advantage of being a houseowner is the freedom it gives people to be able to move to an area where work is available. So naturally, each time we have moved, to Knutsford in Cheshire, then to Letchworth and finally to Hatfield in Hertfordshire, we have always managed to be houseowners.

While I was employed at the South Durham Iron and Steel Company I did a variety of jobs, eventually finishing up with the top job within the crane driving fraternity as a casting-bay crane driver.

From 1952 to 1963 I devoted almost all my spare time to union work on behalf of my colleagues in the industry. Many of the educational functions and meetings I attended were at my own expense. In those days it was very difficult to find employers who would pay for educational courses, whether for industrial needs or trade union activities.

It was in 1956 that I gained my first regional recognition and was elected as a representative on the union's National Negotiating Committee which usually met in London and negotiated pay for the whole industry. My time under Harry Douglass, later to become Lord Douglass of Cleveland, stood me in good stead later in life. My experience and knowledge broadened considerably in the years leading up to 1963.

I was particularly interested in health and safety. The steel industry is a dirty, dangerous and difficult industry to work in. There were a number of occasions when, even as a crane driver, I faced some dangerous situations. Always being an athletic type, I rarely used to climb up the stairs to my crane; instead I had a rope which I shinned up and down like a monkey (something I would not recommend anyone else to do!). On one occasion the fuses in the cab arced; there was a tremendous, blinding flash behind me and in seconds the whole cab was on fire. The men who were working down below climbed up with cans of water in an attempt to quench the flames. By mistake someone had grabbed and thrown a can of paraffin. The cab was a death trap, so I threw out the rope and escaped in the only way possible. I was very lucky on that occasion.

8

In at the Deep End

My growing interest in the work of trade unions was the result of the exploitation of workers that I saw all around me. It was not just the employers who were doing the exploiting. Union negotiators, both full-time and local officials, were interested only in the top-paid workers and not in those doing the less important jobs. When I protested that this was not only unfair but morally wrong, I was told I did not know what I was talking about. Maybe in those days I did not know how to express myself in the clearest terms, but I could see what was right and what was wrong.

Eventually, in 1963, I became a full-time officer in the ISTC as an organizer in Middlesbrough. My divisional officer was Jim Drinkwater, who went on to make his name in the Labour movement. I was extremely pleased with my appointment but, once it became known, the works management approached me and asked if I would stay and become a manager. That was a real challenge, but it was not hard to turn down their offer. If I was to make changes in the way the union conducted its affairs I would have to do it from the inside. Trade unions lose some of their most able men and women to management, who are quick to spot a potential leader. This has robbed the movement as a whole of some of the finest talent around.

I did not tell my wife about the offer, or about my subsequent rejection of it, as I was sure she would think it better to have a position within the company which offered security and status. In fact, I did not finally confess until eighteen years later. Actually, the company later closed down, so even at a materialistic level I probably made the best choice. Certainly I would never have had so much job satisfaction if I had stayed. It has been wonderful to have had the opportunity of helping people with their problems.

For those of us in steel one of the most important milestones was the renationalization of the industry in the 'white heat of the technological revolution' instigated by the government of Harold Wilson in July 1967. It was something we welcomed most warmly. Only if steel became one coherent unit could it achieve the investment programme that British industry so badly needed.

We welcomed especially the appointment of BSC's first chairman, Lord Melchett, who understood the aspirations of working people so well. He wanted a high-productivity, high-earnings industry. So did we. When he died so tragically in his swimming pool I think his ideals died with him. His successors – Sir Monty Finniston and Sir Charles Villiers – uttered the same words, but while we increased productivity year by year, they did very little to ensure that the workers benefited. We had to fight for every penny.

In 1970 I moved to Cheshire to cover that county, Lancashire and North Wales. While I was in Cheshire I came face to face with something that was to haunt me for years to come: a works closure. The works was Irlam in Lancashire and although we fought for the plant we were very much on our own. I shall never forget the look on the faces of the workforce as they filed out of the Irlam gates for the last time.

It struck me then, as it has ever since, that those who speak the loudest about the need to slimline our traditional industries, to rationalize, to shed manpower, ought to stand at factory gates and look the redundant straight in the eye. They might not then speak in such a cavalier fashion. Many people in Britain today seem to have lost their humanity. We talk of lost job opportunities and percentage manpower reductions, never in terms of the suffering that is imposed on fellow human beings.

But looking back at the Irlam experience, I must admit that sometimes trade union hierarchies are also pretty hard to move. When I attended the ISTC Executive to plead for action to defend the plant, warning that if we did not make a stand we would lose one works after the other, I was told by the then general secretary Dai Davies, 'OK, Brother Sirs, you can go back to Irlam and tell them you've made your speech!'

In the Northwest I established a good working relationship with the employers and experienced many good times with the membership. Then, one night I was in a pub with Bob Jones, a local branch officer at the Shotton works. After dealing with a claim his branch was putting to management, he turned to me and said, 'Bill, I bet you will be our next general secretary.' I was amazed. We already had a general secretary, Dai Davies, and an assistant general secretary, Jim Diamond. Was my Shotton colleague somehow psychic? To my surprise, in 1972 Jim Diamond retired prematurely on health grounds and this gave me the opportunity to apply for the position of assistant general secretary. The candidates had first to sit a six-hour written examination at the TUC; then there were oral examinations before the Staffing Subcommittee and the Executive Council. In the event, two assistant secretaries were appointed, myself and Roy Evans, twelve years my junior. In February 1975 I was appointed general secretary designate by the union's twenty-one-strong Executive Council; I was to take over from Dai Davies at the end of the year.

I was glad my position was appointive. Within the trade union movement there has been a great deal of discussion about whether general secretaries should be elected by the membership or appointed by the Executive. After ten years as general secretary I can answer that question very easily. A general secretary should be appointed. He or she is then a member of staff, hired to do the Executive's bidding and fired if his or her performance is not up to scratch. The system makes for efficiency for the faithful enaction of the elected Executive's wishes and therefore for real democracy, and for honest service. An elected general secretary on the other hand has to please this faction or that, always looking over his or her shoulder, and always trimming words so that the most powerful sections of the union are not upset. As an appointed general secretary I felt free to advise as I thought best, to say what I truly believed and take such action as seemed right for the union as a whole. This question is not a matter of right wing versus left wing. One of our strongest left-led unions, TASS, appoints all its officials and the system has enabled it to become one of the most efficient and best-run unions in the country.

Twelve weeks after I became general secretary designate there was a knock on my door; it was Dai Davies's secretary. Would I be going to the next meeting of the TUC Steel Committee? I confirmed that I would. But why this inquiry from a man who, to be honest, had hardly spoken to me since my appointment as assistant general secretary? I had never been able to work out why Dai kept himself to himself and did not share with me the work of the union. Now he wanted to ensure I would be alongside him at the next meeting with British Steel. I was a little suspicious.

When I got to the meeting I found that Dai Davies, who was chairman of the committee, was not there. Neither was the next most senior member of the committee, John Boyd, who represented the craftsmen. The BSC chairman, Sir Monty Finniston, was not there either – nothing surprising about that – but his chief executive, Bob Scholey, gave us some distressing news. He wanted wholesale changes in the industry – and the loss of 20,000 jobs.

I probed Bob Scholey and his colleagues, listened to what they said and then took them to task. We were being presented with what was, in effect, an ultimatum. That was no way to conduct an industry. If the Corporation had problems or wanted to achieve certain savings, then they should share their concerns with us and together we should seek a solution. But the Corporation made it clear that their minds were made up.

When I came out of BSC's headquarters in Grosvenor Place I was met by a host of reporters, cameramen and television and radio interviewers – BSC had already told them the news. Had they told Dai Davies, in advance, I wondered. And was that why he chose not to be at the meeting? I was certainly being dropped in at the deep end.

The following day I went to my office. Still no Dai Davies – he had gone to Luxembourg. The situation was so critical that I accepted the responsibility of calling an Executive Council meeting and invited the Labour Government's Industry Minister, Tony Benn, to attend. I asked him if he could do anything to help us. I have had many disagreements with Tony Benn over the years – he is a prominent spokesman for the Left, I am for moderation – but during those traumatic days he supported me wonderfully. A whole series of meetings with BSC ensued – many of them continuing through the night.

Dai Davies, sensing the difficulties ahead, retired almost immediately and left me with the task of guiding the destinies of my union and of the Steel Committee which I now led.

9

A Diversion:
the EEC Referendum

Apart from the difficulties faced by the steel industry over the threatened closures, my ten years as general secretary of the ISTC began with political turmoil. Britain had a Labour Government committed to a referendum on whether the UK should retain membership of the European Economic Community. It was the Labour Party's way out of a dilemma. The Prime Minister, Harold Wilson, wanted us to stay in, as did most of the Cabinet, but the left of the Party and the 'little Englanders', led by the otherwise admirable Peter Shore, were trying to persuade the government to pull Britain out. Harold's compromise was to hold a referendum and let the people decide.

I was in favour of Britain retaining membership. Industrially she would face a number of problems as part of the EEC, but politically the Community had at last brought together the major nations of Europe which had been on opposing sides in two world wars, thus reducing the possibility of a further Western European conflict.

I was fortunate in that the policy of my union was also to support Britain's membership. We had been part of the European scene since 1951, when we were involved with the birth of the European Coal and Steel Community, and we felt that the industry could benefit from having access to the markets of a united Europe. Thus it was perhaps not surprising that I was asked to join the campaign for a 'yes' vote which included prominent personalities of all political parties. I agreed at once and started touring up and down the country, sharing platforms with the Prime Minister, Reginald Maudling, Roy Jenkins, David Owen and Shirley Williams.

Within the trade union movement the number of general secretaries in favour of Britain's membership of the EEC could be counted on the fingers of one hand, excluding the thumb. Most union leaders fiercely opposed the whole concept of the Common Market. While it was to be expected that Communist and other leaders of the left would oppose our involvement with the EEC, there were also many moderate union leaders who shared their view. At every TUC meeting I attended during and even after the referendum campaign there was considerable hostility towards the EEC and those who supported it. People like myself and Roy Grantham, general secretary of APEX, were in an isolated position.

One campaign meeting stands out in my memory. Two days before the actual referendum I was due to speak at Camden Town Hall with Harold Wilson and Vic Feather, then general secretary of the TUC. There was an angry crowd in the hall, and the press were there in force.

'Here you better have a swig of this,' Vic Feather said, offering me a flask of brandy. I declined; I did not drink brandy. Vic looked at me thoughtfully. 'Well, I think you'll need it tonight.'

Vic led the way to the platform and as soon as we stepped up on the stage the noise erupted. Chanting, shouting, screaming – it never stopped from the moment we set foot on the platform until the moment we left.

'Quiet please – let's have some silence for Harold Wilson, the Prime Minister,' Vic Feather began. His plea was ignored and the row continued.

Harold rose to his feet. The mob fury got worse; it was impossible to hear what Harold was saying. The hall was boiling with hate. One or two things were thrown at the platform; the anti-marketeers were jumping up and down, yelling at the top of their voices. The pro-marketeers present decided to show their feelings and began to chant their favourite slogans. The anti-marketeers jumped up from their seats and started marching up and down the hall, banners flying.

Harold Wilson finished his speech a little prematurely, and it was left to me to wind up. I bawled into the microphone as loudly as I could. I thought I could overcome the crescendo of noise coming from the body of the hall but the attack continued.

As soon as we left the platform, complete silence reigned. There was hardly a murmur. We wondered whether we would have to run the gauntlet of people outside the hall, but the mob had come to disrupt the meeting, nothing more. Their intention was obviously to deflect media interest from what we were saying to the chaos which had ensued. This was my first experience of political activity and I was taken aback by the extremes to which the opposition would go in order to win their fight.

However, our efforts were soon to be vindicated by the referendum result. The British people wished to stay within the Common Market. But although the result was positive, hostility continued for many months afterwards. People like Alan Sapper of the Association of Cinematograph, Television and Allied Technicians were unbelievably hostile, and it shook me how many general secretaries were unwilling to accept the democratic decision of the people.

A lot of this opposition dried up after Jack Jones, the general secretary of the Transport and General Workers Union, intervened. Jack was one of the most vociferous opponents of our membership of the EEC and made a massive contribution to the 'vote no' campaign. But in one of his final meetings as a member of the General Council Jack said it was now time that we accepted the democratic vote. 'The people of this country have spoken, and it is their wish that we should be part of the EEC.' Thereafter we only heard the subdued mumblings of the few who persisted in their attack. Jack Jones is a true man of honour and now works very hard on behalf of Britain's pensioners.

My first experience in the European Economic Community was as a British representative on the Paul Finet Foundation, which is an educational venture giving grants to the children of workers who are killed in the steel and coal industries of Europe.

I then received a government appointment as one of the trade union representatives on the European Coal and Steel Community (ECSC) Consultative Committee. This committee is directly involved in matters affecting production, sales, safety, investment and importing and exporting within the coal and steel industries of the European Community, and comprises producers, consumers and trade unions. With me on the committee were Joe Gormley and National Coal Board chairman Derek Ezra.

Derek Ezra I found to be very pleasant, if somewhat laborious in his presentations, but he nevertheless made sure that he expounded the case for the British coal industry at great length and with great effect. Joe Gormley, then president of the NUM, fought to persuade Europeans that they had a responsibility to formulate a European policy for coal, and what part of that policy should be European investment in the British coal industry – the biggest in Europe.

Over the years I have been involved with a number of different European commissioners, the most effective of whom has been Viscount Davignon, who introduced, after long discussion, a price structure and quota system in an effort to save the European steel industry. The problem the industry faced was world overcapacity due to the increasing number of steel plants being built by the developing world. The world was awash with steel, and as a result employers, particularly the Germans, were undercutting prices in an effort to close down rival European producers. Unfortunately this senseless competition meant, and still means, that the profit ratio in steel is so low that steelworks struggle to survive. Viscount Davignon's greatest triumph was to force the Germans to make a U-turn and accept both quota and price restrictions.

Looking back, I believe Viscount Davignon's plan for steel has worked fairly well. Each of the European producers has reduced capacity and the huge surpluses have been reduced, but Britain has taken a larger cutback than any of the other European member states and for this I blame the present British Government. We have done much more than our fair share – we have cut back too much and sacrificed more than we should. Some ministers have said we have to set an example, and that if the Italians and Belgians are slow to take action, we have to show them the way.

This failure by the present British Government has turned many steelworkers against the whole idea of membership of the EEC. Sadly, at our 1983 Annual Conference the delegates voted to change the union's stance on Europe. The ISTC now favours another referendum to let the British people decide once again whether they wish to stay in or come out. If there were a second referendum I know what I would do. Go on the same platforms, make the same pleas and doubtless face the same barrage of hostility and mob fury.

10

Closure after Closure, Crisis after Crisis

When Tony Benn met the ISTC's Executive Council following BSC's announcement in 1975 that they intended cutting 20,000 jobs, he said he would not and could not accept the solution of the 1930s to cure the problems of the 1970s. He felt, as I did, that the Corporation was attempting to use the short-term recession to expedite long-term plans. He suggested tripartite meetings between BSC, the unions and the government to discuss present problems and future relationships. My Executive welcomed the suggestion warmly.

They also tried to be constructive. After a great deal of discussion, in which they gave a lot of thought to what the Corporation was saying, they accepted a statement I put before them which encapsulated all they felt.

The statement declared that:

1. There should be no suspension of the Guaranteed Week Agreement which guarantees a minimum income even if there is no work and which BSC wanted to end.
2. That tripartite talks proposed by Mr Benn should take place.
3. That the ISTC was prepared to accept, after full consultation at local level, voluntary redundancies where overmanning could be shown to exist.
4. That the only work-sharing the ISTC would accept would be order-sharing between works.
5. That all unnecessary overtime should be eliminated.
6. That the Executive unanimously rejected British Steel's

proposals for works closures and redundancies.

Within a few days the Corporation began exerting pressure at local level, tightening up everywhere and reducing weekend working. Steelworkers began to react and at the Port Talbot works there was a stoppage of our members.

There was a whole series of meetings between BSC and the TUC Steel Committee. Day after day, night after night, the Corporation pressed us to make an agreement on closures and redundancies. Finally we reached an agreement which was presented to my Executive for approval on 30 July 1975. It ran as follows:

1. **Redundancy**
   (a) Employees with less than 12 months' service will be made redundant selectively on a works-by-works basis.
   (b) Employees over 60 years of age will be considered for redundancy on a voluntary and selective basis.
   (c) Jobs which are surplus to requirements will be identified and subjected to negotiations with the appropriate unions before any decision on redundancies is taken.
2. **Guaranteed Working Week Agreement**
   The operation of this Agreement should be the subject of local discussion with a view to reaching agreement to waive its provisions and allow work sharing to take place.
3. **Plant Loading**
   The Corporation will continue to exercise flexibility in the loading of its plants.
4. **Flexibility**
   Subject to local agreement, employees will be ready to work with greater flexibility and adaptability, undertaking work wherever available, irrespective of plant.
5. **Weekend Working**
   The problem of weekend working in those works where there is not a full order book will be the subject of further urgent discussions.

My union reluctantly endorsed this agreement and trusted that improved productivity would lead to improved pay, but our hopes were dashed. At a meeting in November

BSC outlined their very grave financial position for 1975-76, with a forecast loss of £340 million; a similar loss was predicted for 1976-77. They stated that in order to cover these losses they would have to borrow £890 million in order to carry on with their development programme. Although the unions had helped save £76 million in recent months, there would have to be a further saving of £200 million on employment costs. There might have to be some drastic decisions, they said, in early January.

January 1976 came – and so did the iron fist. BSC wanted to scrap the Guaranteed Week Agreement and to change manning levels yet again. On 8 January we met all day. On 9 and 10 January we met for thirty-two hours. On 22 and 23 January we met for twenty-one hours. The agreement we finally reached was endorsed by all the steel unions, including my own which held a special Executive meeting to receive the report.

It was during these marathon negotiations that I began to have some sympathy with the industrial correspondents of the media. The issue was of national importance and received nationwide coverage, but in order for them to get the story the correspondents had to stay in Grosvenor Place, or in the pub next door, during the whole proceedings, both day and night!

Within any set of negotiations there are adjournments when private discussions can take place. During our talks Bob Scholey, BSC's chief executive, kept insisting that he wanted a copperbottomed agreement. If he said it once he must have said it a dozen times. Eventually a frustrated Hector Smith, general secretary of the National Union of Blastfurnacemen, responded by pulling down his trousers and exposing his posterior. 'That's the only copperbottomed agreement you'll get from me!' he declared.

The agreement we eventually reached, allowing for further flexibility and demanning, was to be the subject of heated discussion over the coming months. But in the long run the unions had to recognize the need for interchangeability and flexibility in order to survive.

Following the agreement of 23 January came years of

continual pressure on myself and on the unions as BSC sought to reduce capacity by closing the older, less efficient plants. Decisions had already been taken about the closure or partial closure of plants like Clyde Iron, Hartlepool, East Moors and Ebbw Vale before I became general secretary. Their lives had been extended for a few years – until about 1980 – by a tripartite meeting chaired by Lord Beswick of the Department of Industry in 1974. One by one, these works closed down, as I shall explain.

But Sir Monty Finniston was not around to see them go. The friction between him and Tony Benn had become very serious, and although the press expected Sir Monty to resign, in fact the government declined to renew his contract.

Sir Monty Finniston had been an effervescent chairman of British Steel, a pleasant character and an enjoyable companion, but he was sometimes rather headstrong. He liked to do his own thing and go his own way, and sometimes got it wrong.

I remember the famous occasion when there was some debate among BSC's senior executives as to whether to have one or two new direction plants (which make iron directly from iron ore) at Hunterston. The internal debate was filmed by BBC Television and was shown in the 'Decisionmakers' series. Viewers saw Monty, who wanted two plants, being opposed by one of his directors, but he badgered away at the others and eventually achieved what he wanted – Board approval for two plants. I felt that was unwise and said so, but Monty persisted. The plants were installed, were hardly used, proved uneconomic, and stood for years as monuments to Monty's folly.

But overall Monty was a great engineer, an innovator, a powerful driving force. Unfortunately he was a poor salesman; he let BSC's marketing performance deteriorate and has to be strongly criticized for that.

There was great speculation about who should succeed him and I was certainly anxious to see someone in that position who would co-operate with the workforce to achieve savings and increase efficiency rather than enter into continual confrontation. Workers want to work in an efficient organization; they like to be part of a team that makes profits which can then be reinvested in the business as well as give the Exchequer some welcome finance. I wish more people would realize that. Workers want to work *with* management, but too often British managers assume the worse and take foolish, bullheaded action. But who was Finniston's successor to be? Who was there who could come in as chairman of British Steel and succeed with us?

I spoke to Eric Varley, Tony Benn's successor as Industry Minister, regarding the appointment. Eric asked my opinion and whether I had any names to offer to him. At that stage I did not have any recommendations to make, but said I would certainly think about it. Soon afterwards Eric saw me again and indicated that he now had someone in mind. A day later I received a telephone call from Will Camp, British Steel's brilliant director of public relations. It was he who created BSC's highly successful 'Steel Appeal' campaign which boosted sales of all steel products. I knew him to be utterly committed to steel and to the concept of state ownership of the industry; he was probably the finest publicist British industry has seen since the Second World War, but he had been fired from BSC after a row over the help he had given to Harold Wilson during the 1970 general election campaign which Harold lost and Ted Heath won.

'Nice to hear from you, Will. What can I do for you?' I asked.

'Can you come and have lunch with me, Bill? I would like to discuss the chairmanship of BSC with you and bring someone along to meet you.'

We met at the Gay Hussar restaurant in Soho and Will introduced me to Peter Parker, who was being considered as the next chairman of British Rail. We talked a great deal, and then Will asked me how I would feel about Peter becoming BSC's next chairman. Well, I liked the idea very much. Peter Parker was an enlightened industrialist, a supporter of the Labour Government and a businessman with a brilliant track record.

After further discussion I was even more impressed with Peter Parker, but I had to warn them that it was probably too late, although I promised to speak to Eric Varley as soon as I got back to the office. I reached Eric later in the day but unfortunately the appointment had been made. A short time afterwards Britain heard that BSC's next chief was to be the merchant banker, Sir Charles Villiers. I often wonder what might have happened to our industry had I met Will Camp and Peter Parker a few days earlier.

In June 1978 the ISTC Annual Conference was held at Scarborough, and we decided to invite Sir Charles to speak to us, along with Eric Varley. Sir Charles was a man of great charm, a liberal who had a strong belief in industrial democracy. He spoke about the need for better co-operation in industry – something we could applaud. When he got back to London, however, he announced that the Corporation, without any consultation at all, was to close the Bilston works.

There was uproar at our conference. It was the first time during my period as general secretary that I saw a reaction against closure that might result in strike action. My Executive Council had a private meeting and decided to recommend that, unless BSC withdrew its proposal, there should be a strike. Conference fully endorsed this and a resolution calling for a strike was carried unanimously with great fervour and acclamation.

On 16 August after the conference, the Executive Council met in London and I reported to them that I had sent a telegram to Sir Charles Villiers informing him of our decision to hold a national strike unless the Corporation withdrew its Bilston proposal. I also approached Eric Varley, urging him to intervene. As a result, BSC withdrew and we entered into negotiations.

It was then that one of the dirtiest tricks ever was played on us. Bilston had one single blast furnace and the blastfurnacemen who manned it were persuaded to allow the furnace to be taken off so that a 'repair' could be carried out. Whether there was any real urgency about the repair I shall never know, but the blast furnace was never brought back into operation and I do not think the Corporation ever intended that it should.

With the blast furnace off, the pressure to close Bilston was very strong. Nevertheless, the workforce, backed by my union, put up a tremendous struggle for survival. They even went in to put the furnace right themselves, but it was not possible to order, authorize and pay for spares, and the workforce began to realize the writing was on the wall.

I led a delegation to see Viscount Davignon, EEC Commissioner for Industry in Brussels. The meeting was held in the Berlaymont building. The commissioners are all housed on the top floor and we met Viscount Davignon in his own office. We discussed all aspects of the Bilston closure, pointing out that over the years the plant had consistently made a profit, was tightly manned and had no industrial problems whatsoever. It was being closed simply because BSC wanted to reduce the number of units it controlled. The Corporation hoped to load up other units in Sheffield with the orders normally processed at Bilston. This was a policy I had always condemned; customers rarely keep their orders with British Steel once their favourite plant has been closed. Usually those orders go abroad. Viscount Davignon promised to raise the issue with the Government. But at the time the Labour Government, although concerned, was battling on so many other fronts that the problems of the steel industry failed to get the attention it deserved, and besides, Viscount Davignon did not press them particularly hard.

Finally, on 11 April 1979, a special meeting of the ISTC's Executive discussed the situation and declared: 'We have come reluctantly to the conclusion that it will be in the interests of all concerned to ask the general secretary to involve himself in negotiations that would result in severance terms with the Corporation that will give employees a long-term cushioning effect against further unemployment.'

I therefore led a team to negotiate redundancy terms; if that was what we had to do we would do it well and get the highest payouts we could. Deep down, I was angry – and so were most other steelworkers. My members could understand the shutdown of loss-making plants, but not good profitable plants like Bilston.

BSC had announced the premature closure of the Clyde Iron Works in Scotland; it should have survived until 1980 under the Beswick agreements. I again appealed to the Minister, and the government *did* do something they thought would help us. They allowed the British Steel Corporation to make much bigger redundancy payments to those workers who accepted early works closure and early redundancy. But the offer of still greater golden handshakes was the last thing we needed. I knew in my heart that now we would never successfully fight a closure, even if the workers agreed to give it a go.

BSC of course, was delighted. At Clyde Iron they went over our heads direct to the workforce and the lure of a few thousand pounds severance pay was enough to make the majority of the workers vote for acceptance of BSC's offer.

Then we began facing difficulties at Hartlepool where the blast furnaces had been shut down 'temporarily' and where our members had little or no work and were receiving poor guaranteed earnings. Our members, and those of other unions, wanted out. They had heard about the golden givaways at Clyde Iron and they wanted the same treatment. Soon we began receiving requests from local Hartlepool branches for a meeting to discuss the possibilities of selling to the Corporation the remaining period of time that the plant was due to operate. After lengthy discussions the Corporation offered increased severance pay based on service and earnings, which our local delegation, after some hours deliberation, accepted. A mass meeting of Hartlepool workers accepted BSC's offer. This agreement was being closely monitored by those other plants in BSC which had a fixed closure date.

I was then asked to go to the East Moors works in Cardiff to meet delegates of the whole workforce. When I arrived the delegates said they wanted to discuss an eight-point plan which, if accepted by BSC, meant agreement for earlier closure. So once again the offer of high redundancy payments, which could amount to over £20,000 in some cases, proved to be too much for us.

How *can* you get workers, many of them in their fifties, some of them in debt, others needing a new car or new furniture or a holiday, to turn down huge sums of money and instead fight the employers with tough, sustained industrial and political action? The fact is, you cannot.

Next came Ebbw Vale. 'Would you like the cash?' B S C asked the local workforce. Put like that, of course they would. Just as East Moors had accepted a better package than that offered at Hartlepool, so Ebbw Vale accepted a package better than that at East Moors.

I then received a request from the workers at Shelton, and we had to take our negotiating circus to that plant, where we did a similar deal.

Closure, closure, closure. And crisis, crisis, crisis. But it was now 1979, and worse was to come.

11

The Social Contract – Why It Failed

At a time when there was turmoil in steel, there was turmoil in the Labour and trade union movement too.

I was elected to the General Council of the TUC in September 1975. At that time the General Council included very prominent figures such as Alf Allen, General Secretary of the Shopworkers' Union, USDAW, Tom Jackson, General Secretary of the Union of Communication Workers which represented the post office workers, Hugh Scanlon of the AUEW, and Jack Jones. I always got on well with Jack Jones who helped me as a 'new boy', and although his policies were sometimes a lot farther to the left than my own, he is a man I have always respected. Tom Jackson, Alf Allen and I worked rather more closely, and I found them to be very fine men of principle and understanding who were striving for a more traditional approach within the Labour Party and the TUC. They were also leaders with imagination and sound logic.

The first major issue I became involved in with both my union and the TUC was the Social Contract. The government, led by Harold Wilson, was suffering the effects of the oil crisis of 1973 and having to cope with inflation fuelled by cost-of-living increases ranging up to 22 per cent. The oil crisis is blamed even today for the nation's woes. How hard it must have hit the Labour administration at that time. Harold Wilson and his ministers wanted to involve the trade unions in coping with this situation and they proposed a Social Contract under which the government and the unions agreed the level of pay increases, price rises and other issues. In my view it was one of the finest agreements ever made between the unions and the government of the day. Jack Jones was a leading figure in promoting the trade union side of the Contact, and I sometimes thought that it would never have succeeded but for him.

The result of the first year of the Social Contract was to reduce inflation to around 13 per cent. The unions had made a tremendous contribution, and Britain's lower-paid workers did particularly well from the first year's operation.

We in steel, however, were facing complex problems. As an industry in a state of continual change, we have always negotiated at works level any improvements in pay resulting from changing practices, new technology, manning levels and so on. The Social Contract required that we cease these local negotiations. We did not like it, but we followed the lead set by the TUC and complied.

I led a delegation from my union to the TUC's Financial and General Purposes Committee and put to them the case for dispensation in productivity and change-of-practice deals. We were unsuccessful and had to accept the TUC's decision.

In 1978, after three years of the Social Contract, our pay patterns and differentials were in a mess and the TUC itself was beginning to fragment. Things had not been helped by the unexpected retirement of Harold Wilson and the emergence of Jim Callaghan as the new Leader of the Labour Party, and therefore the new Prime Minister. He had all the worsening problems of a minority government. 1978 was also Jack Jones's last year as general secretary of the TGWU and this time he failed to persuade his union to go along with an extension of the Social Contract agreement. Jim Callaghan was to address the 1978 TUC Congress in September. Would he try to win a new lease of life for the Contract? Or would he name the date of the next general election, which we anticipated would be held during October.

We were surprised, and I think most of us were disappointed, that he did not announce the date of the general election. We felt that with the government's understanding with the trade unions it would have been a good time to go to the country. Jim obviously felt otherwise. Instead, he gathered a few TUC representatives around him and sounded them out about the possibility of a further round of the Social Contract.

At the October meeting of the General Council we were told that our representatives were nearing agreement with the Callaghan Government. But, I asked, would there be any concessions for those workers, such as steelworkers, who were increasing productivity without being able to improve their pay through local productivity deals? Productivity in steel was improving rapidly. If the workers were not to share in the benefits that accrued, they would be lost to Labour for ever. If the Social Contract was abandoned at some future date, the employers were not going to say, 'Hey, we had all these changes but you couldn't take the money. Have the cash now.' I tried to make my views clear.

We seemed to be getting nowhere in our discussions, so I had to say that unless productivity agreements could be built into the new Social Contract, the ISTC could not go along with it. I also felt that we ought to be able to express our concern to Jim Callaghan direct – why could he not talk to the whole General Council?

At the November meeting of the General Council the Economic Committee presented a draft agreement and we were asked to approve. The draft made no mention of our special problems; all I had said had been ignored. I found this difficult to understand, so I said I would vote against it. This pleased the left, which had never really wanted the Social Contract or any other form of incomes control.

There was also some confusion about the view of the new general secretary of the TGWU, Moss Evans. He had been one of the small team preparing the draft agreement with Jim Callaghan; indeed, he had supported the draft. But now the word was going round that he no longer favoured a further incomes policy; he wanted to return to free collective bargaining. I supposed we could ask him where he

With Prince Charles at the ISTC conference in 1979

At the TUC conference in Brighton, 1976. Hugh Scanlon sits behind

Bill Sirs, flanked by Hector Smith of the Blastfurnacemen, Jim Callaghan and, far right, Les Bramley, during the steel strike in 1980

Visiting pickets at Redcar in January 1980

In Brighton, September 1984, on the way to TUC conference and just before angry crowds advanced

Bill Sirs sits amidst derelict engineering factory buildings near Hartlepool in 1983

Typically pugnacious. Bill Sirs at his ISTC desk in 1982

Bill Sirs aged eleven (*left*) and dapper at nineteen (*right*)

Bill Sirs, centre, with friends Matthew and Alex Kelly from Middleton, in 1937

Left: The family in 1954. Bill and Joan Sirs, with Margaret and John

Below: Bill and Joan Sirs with daughter Margaret and granddaughters Joanne and Victoria in 1977

Above: The TUC took on the Industrial Correspondents in 1982. Bill Sirs opens the batting in Brighton and John Richards of the *Daily Telegraph* keeps wicket

Right: Running at night during the steel strike, 1980

"What, Mr Sirs! Don't you want to celebrate the anniversary of the Tolpuddle Martyrs by being a nice bonfire?"

How Cummings depicted Bill Sirs' conflict with Arthur Scargill during the miners' strike, 1985

stood, but he was not at this crucial meeting.

When we took a vote it was fifteen for, fifteen against. Tom Jackson, the president, had to declare the proposal lost and the Social Contract, unfortunately, was no more.

I reported my actions to my Executive Council who endorsed my action.

In the debate that ensued across the country, some observers said that the government might have succeeded if it had promised to build into the Contract a general increase of more than the 5 per cent which Chancellor Denis Healey was pondering. I am sure the government could have been pushed to 7 or 8 per cent, but for me and my union that was not the point. We needed a contract that was flexible enough to accommodate productivity agreements.

The government, of course, was terribly disappointed about the outcome of the General Council meeting. I explained to Jim Callaghan very clearly that we still supported the concept of a prices and incomes policy and that we had not joined the group of left-led unions!

So now we had that wonderful beast, free collective bargaining. No one has ever really explained to me what free collective bargaining is. What is free? What is collective? And what is bargaining if you are in an industry in decline with no bargaining counters? Essentially, it seems to me, free collective bargaining means the powerful being given free rein to grab all the goodies, while the rest – like the nurses, school dinner ladies and agricultural workers – scramble for the crumbs.

One union that was pleased to get back free collective bargaining was NUPE – the National Union of Public Employees. Yet under the Social Contract its low-paid members had made remarkable progress. NUPE, sensitive to this criticism, was determined that with free collective bargaining it would get substantial increases (irrespective of whether the government could afford them!) and soon disputes were breaking out all over the place.

So we approached the Winter of Discontent. Council workers went on strike and the press had a field day. They reported only the most extreme cases – the caretaker who would not open the school gates so that children had to be turned away, the cemetery workers who would not bury the dead, the ambulance that did not go to an emergency.

In February 1979, in the midst of all this chaos, the TUC General Council went to 10 Downing Street to see Jim Callaghan. I suggested to David Basnett, who as chairman was leading the delegation, that the General Council should agree to accept the same rules as those that apply in the coal and steel industries: when there is a strike, safety services always operate. There was no response.

Jim Callaghan tried hard to persuade the General Council to do something to bring some order to our daily lives, but to no avail. The Winter of Discontent swirled on, Jim Callaghan went to the country, and Margaret Thatcher became Britain's first woman Prime Minister.

Although I was partly responsible for ending the Social Contract and ushering in the winter of strife that led to the downfall of the Labour Government, I could have acted no other way. However, I still firmly believe in an incomes policy supported by all sections of the community.

When, as I wish, Neil Kinnock forms the next Labour Government, I hope that the unions and the government will get together to fashion a new agreement embracing not just incomes and prices but the aspirations of the country and of the 10 million trade unionists within the country. Together, we can do great things. Without each other, there is very little we can do.

If I am remembered for my part in the Social Contract collapse, I hope I am also remembered in trade union circles for something a little more constructive. I have always been interested in health and the environment, and have long considered smoking harmful not only to those who indulge, but their friends, family and colleagues around them. For this reason I became involved in voluntary work for the British Empire Cancer Campaign Committee.

Each time the TUC Congress was held at Blackpool the chairman had, at some stage, to appeal to the delegates to smoke less. The atmosphere became thick with cancerous fumes. In Brighton the air is a little clearer as the hall is larger! At the beginning of the first session of the 1980 Congress I moved an emergency motion that there should be no smoking. A conflagration followed.

While moving the motion I was interrupted by a delegate who raised a point of order. The delegate, a rather heavily built woman member of the Tobacco Workers Union, dashed down to the rostrum from the back of the hall. When she got to the microphone she was puffing and blowing. I stooped down to help her onto the rostrum; she could hardly catch her breath, effectively making my point for me! Tom Jackson, the president, called for a hand vote – and declared the motion carried (although it cannot have been by a very large margin). A lot of delegates, of course, did not like it one bit and the protests rumbled on through the rest of the week.

The following year I again moved an emergency motion and the president, Terry Parry of the Fire Brigades Union, allowed me to speak. Terry was a great supporter of the no-smoking campaign. His own smoking in earlier years had left him with bad circulation in the legs, and he had pledged himself to do everything he could to persuade people to stop – or, better still, not to take up the habit in the first place. Once again, we won the day. Then one of the delegates asked for a card vote, when each union casts the vote of the total number of members it has affiliated to the TUC. Terry Parry, who was a wonderfully humorous man, responded by saying that cards do not smoke, and that was the end of the intervention.

The following year, when the General Council was discussing the programme for Congress, David Basnett complained about my having three bites of the cherry. Each union can move only two motions, yet here was I, the general secretary of the ISTC, each year moving an emergency resolution on smoking. This was a view the Council accepted and I was therefore obliged to go to my union and ask them to support me by allowing me to use one of their motions to create a *permanent* no-smoking policy for the TUC. My own Executive was split almost 50-50 between smokers and non-smokers – but I received support from some of the smokers who said that although they were not prepared to change their own habits they recognized the strength of the argument – that we had to prevent young people from taking up smoking. On that basis I got permission from my union to use one of their motions. At the next Congress I now had ten minutes to outline the dangers of smoking – it was a great opportunity. Naturally I was opposed by the Tobacco Workers Union, but when the vote was taken the motion was carried by almost two to one.

We also won a ban on smoking at the Labour Party Conference.

The TUC has since gone further. The Social Insurance Committee decided that there would be no smoking at all TUC committee meetings. One man voting alongside me was Arthur Scargill – it must have been the only time he agreed with me about anything! But thank you, Arthur.

I do not think Len Murray, when general secretary of the TUC, was too pleased about what I had done. Len used to like smoking a cigar during meetings, and I believe that Norman Willis would much prefer to be smoking a cigarette. I am certainly very grateful to those smokers who were prepared to help me achieve these changes in policy. They did so, I think, for the sake of future generations.

I received sackfuls of letters from both smokers and non-smokers. Some of these who wrote to me were very angry indeed. How dare I take away people's freedom to smoke! To which I can only reply, how dare they take away the freedom of the rest of us to breathe clean, clear air.

12

Corby, Consett and Prince Charles

The defeat of Jim Callaghan and the arrival of Margaret Thatcher at No. 10 in 1979 heralded a new competitive, combatant era not only for our nation but for British industry. The Prime Minister was determined to 'take on the unions'. And she thought she would start with steel.

The long struggle to keep iron and steelmaking at the Shotton works in North Wales – which we had been waging since 1972 – ended when, after renewed pressure exerted upon them, the workforce decided to allow the steelmaking operation to finish and to accept welcome financial investment in the steel-coating plant, which since then has proved enormously successful.

But BSC's decision to end steelmaking at Corby in Northamptonshire came as a shock. BSC wanted the plant to import steel slabs and roll them into pipes and tubes. Yet Corby was sitting on locally mined iron ore which was the feedstock for the blast furnaces.

We embarked on a programme of resistance and called in two professors of accountancy at Warwick University to help us. There was initially some objection from a few members of the TUC Steel Committee when the professors joined us as part of our negotiating team, but their presence was of great benefit. I believe trade unions ought to make more use of the many experts around. We need to use professional planners, analysts, statisticians, publicity and marketing specialists in the same way we all use lawyers now.

Tensions were running very high in Corby, with marches and demonstrations taking place every week. Then, quite suddenly, we began to be faced with requests and demands to negotiate closure. This was once again due in the main to the high redundancy payments on offer. People were also fed up. They had no faith or trust in BSC's management any more, and certainly felt no loyalty. The fight that began so hopefully therefore simply fizzled out. Steelmaking at Corby ceased, leaving the tube and pipemaking section intact.

At the same time we were dealing with the proposed closure of the Consett works. BSC had tried to close Consett earlier, but we had successfully resisted them. Eventually the management came up with a package. If we co-operated with a big cost-cutting exercise, we could save the plant. So we co-operated, and the savings were made. But that had no influence on British Steel, which decided to close Consett anyway and transfer the order book to the Normanby Park works in Scunthorpe.

We felt we had been cheated and badly let down. For the town of 20,000, the steelworks was the main employer. It was making a profit, it had a good labour force with very few industrial relations problems, and it produced an excellent quality material. Furthermore, we made it quite clear to BSC that we were prepared to offer plans for further improvements and a further reduction in costs. The arguments we had at our disposal for the retention of steelmaking in Consett were quite considerable, and we began to deploy these arguments very forcibly with the British Steel Corporation and in the press.

In the main we had a tremendously loyal, trustworthy membership with first-class work attitudes at Consett. It came somewhat as a surprise to me when I began to receive criticism for putting up a struggle to keep Consett open. One representative of the National Union of Blastfurnace-men said that I had no right to be fighting against the closure proposals, and one of my own branches in the steelmaking area wrote in to ask for closure negotiations. It was again the lure of high redundancy payments. I replied that we were only interested in saving jobs and saving the works at Consett.

It was during a break in negotiations with BSC in Middlesbrough that I learned that there were groups in Consett who were actually talking to management and agreeing with the closure proposals. The folly of such behaviour is hard to understand. As I explained to delegates at the negotiations, the position at Consett was rather different from that of many other areas. There was no alternative work. There was no alternative industry, and the likelihood of persuading industralists to go to Consett, taking into consideration its remote position, was very limited. Anyone could foresee members being unemployed for many years if the plant should close.

The campaign being waged by the many excellent men and women in the plant, many of them local councillors and community leaders who knew only too well what a tragedy it would be if the works closed, was spirited and imaginative. I well remember their long journey to London in a special train, their march through London where they won the immediate sympathy of the people of the capital, and their intensive, intelligent lobbying of Parliament.

Then I suddenly received a strange request from a firm of management consultants. Would I meet one of their number to discuss a buy-out of the Consett steel plant? I was excited by the proposal and agreed to a meeting. There was, I was told, a group of businessmen, many of whom were suppliers to the Consett works, who were determined not to let the plant go down, both for humane and for economic reasons. Those selling goods and services to the plant stood to lose a lot of custom.

I was asked to consider two things. First, would I help them in persuading BSC to sell and, secondly, would the ISTC be prepared to invest some money in the venture. I said I would be prepared to help and so far as investment by ISTC was concerned we would have to see. If the project really did look like taking off, then I would certainly be prepared to recommend some investment to my Executive Council, but the consortium of businessmen had to proceed on the assumption that no union money would be involved.

I asked the names of the members of the consortium, but was told that would be breaking confidentiality at this stage. Some of the companies, which were very large, feared that British Steel, which would not be pleased about a bid because it wanted to transfer Consett's order book to the Normanby Park works, might act against them and deny them work and contracts in other parts of the Corporation. However, I was told the name of the chairman of the group, the head of a well-known supplier to BSC, and that satisfied me, particularly after a colleague who subsequently met him confirmed that he was involved and hopeful of a successful outcome.

The problem was that British Steel, which became alarmed at hearing on the grapevine that a consortium was holding meetings prior to any bid, accelerated its closure timetable. After discussion with the management consultants, I decided that the only thing that could stop BSC in its tracks would be full public knowledge of the bid the consortium was trying to put together.

None of the businessmen would agree to put their head over the parapet, so the representative of the management consultants and I held a press conference to reveal what was happening behind the scenes. Television, radio and newspapers stampeded to the press conference at a Bloomsbury hotel. Here was a steel story with a difference. A group of businessmen who did not want to close a works but were actually trying to put money into one. The consultant explained that a consortium of some twenty businesses was being formed and that discussions were taking place between their principals and their advisers with a view to making a bid for the steel plant. If the bid was successful the plant would be kept open, would receive further investment, and its order book would be retained and – because of the consortium's marketing experience – expanded.

A buzz of excitement went round the room. In turn, I publicly appealed to British Steel not to act too hastily and to give the consortium time to put together and submit its bid. What the press wanted to know, of course, was who the twenty businesses were. 'I'm sorry,' the management consultant declared, 'we really are unable to give you that information. The situation is very sensitive indeed. All I can say is that the group is sound and substantial.'

As the days drew on, however, the press kept asking the same question: who were the mystery twenty? The *Sunday Times* was particularly anxious to get hold of the story.

A week passed, then another, then another, and I began to get concerned. The management consultants assured me all was well, but I knew it would not be long before B S C turned out the Consett furnaces. Indeed, I received a private message from Grosvenor Place telling me exactly that. They dare not do anything too hastily – the public exposure of the possible bid had seen to that – but now that they had persuaded large sections of the workforce to go for the redundancy payoffs they wanted to do the deed.

I received another message. The furnaces would be off in five days' time – on the coming Monday – a week before the consortium was due to have its final meeting before putting the bid. My press and public relations adviser Keith Bill and I considered that only one thing could stop B S C now: a strong editorial in the *Sunday Times* denouncing any move to cut off Consett's lifeblood while the bid was being finalized. The *Sunday Times*, under the editorship of Harry Evans, was then at its peak. It was powerful, campaigning – and feared in Whitehall.

Keith contacted the *Sunday Times* and went to talk to the editor of their business section. He confirmed he was interested in the story and would do what he could to help. Then Keith saw Harry Evans, who declared his sympathy for the Consett community – he came from the Northeast himself – but wanted to see the list of the twenty businesses and to speak to the individuals concerned to check that the story stood up. Then he would run a piece.

'An editorial,' Keith said. Harry Evans agreed.

Keith and I conferred briefly; we now had to get the list. We would demand it from the consultants; if it was not forthcoming, then we would publicly withdraw our support for the project and declare, reluctantly and sadly, that we could see no chance of the works now being saved.

This tactic worked. After much to-ing and fro-ing and agonizing the management consultants and three members of the consortium met Keith Bill and handed over the twenty names. 'But there won't be any public exposure or any contact from the *Sunday Times*, will there?' one of the businessmen asked. Keith did not reply.

The following Saturday morning Keith Bill received a telephone call at his home from Harry Evans. 'I'm sorry,' he was told, 'the consortium is not as solid as I hoped. Of the fourteen we've spoken to, only eight or nine are at this stage absolutely committed. There's not enough big money there yet, so we can't do our piece.' Evans was genuinely upset. So were we. We had this one outside chance of being able to save the plant, but it was not to be.

That Sunday the *Sunday Times*, with our blessing, ran a piece nonetheless declaring that the consortium was not strong enough to win the works. Consett's fate was sealed.

I was impressed by our dealings with the *Sunday Times* – they were scrupulous and fair. But I have always thought more of the media than most of my colleagues. Working journalists I have always found to be trustworthy; not once have I had a confidence broken. If you try to be open and honest with them, I have found that they will be honest in their dealings with you.

The majority of the workers at Consett had indeed by this time agreed to take the money and go. I think the reason for this can be seen if one looks at the age structure of the work force. Many of the workers were long-serving, experienced men, and those who were aged sixty-two would receive 90 per cent of their earnings for two years after their enforced retirement. Why should they want to stay? If they were sixty or fifty-five or fifty they would receive similar, scaled-down, benefits. Most of the workers would receive pensions, help from the European Coal and Steel Community and about £10,000 as a lump sum. Some received £20,000. Never before had they been offered so much money. The pressure to take redundancy must have been, for many, irresistible and I can understand this, although I am saddened by it.

In my last year as general secretary of the union I went back to Consett to present to Derwentside council a memento – a framed picture of a steelworks in the 1920s. The closure in my view was a tragedy which we should never forget, and if anyone would care to count the costs of closure as against the costs of continued operation, I am sure this would reveal good reasons for continued operation. Eighty-five per cent of Consett's school leavers never find jobs. For them there are only the youth training schemes with nothing to follow afterwards. I think as a nation we have failed this community miserably – a community which in the past has contributed so much to the British economy.

Shotton, Corby, Consett. . . . In view of the seriousness of the position my Executive invited BSC chief executive Bob Scholey to meet us, with his colleagues, to discuss the future policy of British Steel. When would the cutbacks end? And what was the meaning of a letter he had sent informing me that there would have to be radical changes in our next round of pay talks? Bob Scholey had written to say that our next national pay negotiations should fall into two parts – a 'modest' national increase and anything else based on self-financing demanning deals. It seemed premature. Was he trying to pre-empt the national negotiations? Was there to be no national increase to meet inflation? Something told me we were heading for trouble.

Before we met Bob Scholey we called together our Central Negotiating Committee and put forward a claim for a 'substantial' wage increase without stating a figure.

We met BSC on 30 November 1979. Bob Scholey said that he wished to be frank with the Executive Council. He outlined the problems facing BSC, declaring that sales were too low and overcapacity too high, and the Corporation therefore had to reduce its cost base, which meant, of course, further job losses and streamlining. Gordon Sambrook, BSC sales and marketing chief at that time, outlined the commercial position and said the Corporation was withdrawing £2 million of orders for sheet and plate from the export market because of the poor prices it was able to secure. This would mean, said Scholey, the elimination of approximately 10,000 jobs.

We were utterly dismayed. Here was the Corporation still going down the vicious spiral. Every time they cut back production they spread the overheads more thinly with the result that each tonne of steel had to carry even more of the central costs. Thus steel became too expensive and did not sell. So what did they do? Cut production yet again to try to recoup money – and so the sorry merry-go-round went on.

If only they had drive, verve and vision. I yearned for someone like John Powell to be at the helm, the man who headed first Ebbw Vale and then the Shotton steelworks. He was a born leader who loved his own people, and they loved him. He had a great vision of working with his people as a team in a determined attempt to beat the competition, especially the foreign competition. He showed the way, he cut costs, he improved performance – and he never let his people down. This last is why BSC had to move him from his plants before it could shut its steelmaking activities down. John would not stand for it! He is now usefully and busily engaged in the Welsh Sports Council and other bodies. That was the kind of man we needed then and, I am sure, will need again.

In contrast, it was a miserable lot who confronted us that bleak November day. . . . We criticized very strongly what Gordon Sambrook and Bob Scholey had said. 'If we go on like this,' one of our number declared, 'we'll have no British industry left, let alone steel.'

He was right, of course. Since 1979 we have lost a third of our British industries and this process has been encouraged by a government which sees our nation as one which will survive on tourism, banking and insurance. Our industrial competitors overseas must be laughing.

My Executive, after hearing what Bob Scholey and his colleagues had to say, decided to take immediate action against further steel closures. On 8 November 1979, at a meeting of the TUC Steel Committee, I moved the following proposals:

1. An embargo on all overtime work in the public sector.
2. A national demonstration to lobby Parliament, during which period there should be a twenty-four hour national steel stoppage.
3. Further selective strikes in the steel industry.
4. The withdrawal of union representatives from all the consultative machinery.
5. No further negotiations on severance and redundancy payments.

I thought this package of action would at least cause the Corporation to think twice. To my astonishment the other steel unions were not prepared to back the ISTC proposals. The meeting broke up after hostile views had been exchanged between some delegations.

The ISTC then made approaches to Jim Callaghan, now Leader of the Opposition, and discussed with him and the TUC the problems that our industry faced. Jim Callaghan said he would introduce a special emergency debate on the problems of the industry in Parliament, and the Secretary of State for Industry, Jim Prior, would be informed of all the developments including the possibility of strike action. Callaghan proved immensely helpful. He must have felt somewhat bitter after the collapse of the Social Contract, but since then we had repaired and renewed our relationship.

Harold Wilson and Jim Callaghan had something in common: a warmth towards their fellow human beings, an ability to listen, contribute and encourage. And, funnily enough, they both said the same thing to me. I was walking down one of the corridors in the House of Commons to speak to the Industry Secretary one day in 1976 when I met Harold, then Prime Minister, who, after a brief chat about the problems facing steel, said, 'I'll tell you one thing, Bill. I wouldn't have your job for a pension!' And that from a man faced with all the difficulties of the nation! Two years later, in 1978, I was walking down the same corridor to see the same Industry Secretary, Eric Varley, when I met Jim

Callaghan, who was then Prime Minister. Once again we had a chat, and Jim used exactly the same words as had Harold Wilson. 'I wouldn't have your job for a pension'.

Now, as I contemplated what was before us towards the end of 1979 – a new hardline Conservative Government, a demand for a further 10,000 redundancies, and trouble on pay – I felt the same thing. Why was I doing it? I suppose the answer was the same as when I took my first humble trade union post as a young man in South Durham: because I wished to serve. The responsibilities now were enormous, but I could not run away from them.

There had been one bright spot in 1979 – our annual conference in Bournemouth. I had invited Prince Charles to address the conference and, to my delight, he accepted. It would be the first time any member of the royal family had attended a trade union conference to speak to delegates. Of course, I was slightly apprehensive. Some of our delegates were anti-monarchist and probably would resent having the Prince in our midst. And Prince Charles had promised to field questions. What might be asked, and what might be said? However, I need not have worried, for the Prince came up to join us on our platform without any fuss or ceremony and listened to our own domestic debates for nearly two hours.

I noticed that he made occasional notes and indeed he questioned me afterwards about a number of the problems we were having. When the time came for him to speak he talked enthusiastically about the contribution trade unions make to society, and of the need for commitment, participation and worker involvement in decision making. It was a first-class performance, full of humour, wit and common sense and all the delegates warmed to him.

Then came question time. One of our most outspoken, controversial left-wingers rose to speak. The Prince, he said, had a mother who loved and raced horses. Could Prince Charles give the conference any racing tips? The conference burst into laughter, and the Prince joined in.

After more questions, the Prince made a powerful speech on the need for co-operation in British industry and he was given a standing ovation. Every delegate, I noticed, was on his or her feet.

Our president, Les Bramley, made a formal presentation to our visitor, and then the Prince joined us for lunch, meeting and speaking with as many delegates as possible.

It struck me afterwards that the Prince had a good grasp of trade union history and of the apsirations and concerns of unions in the twentieth century. Obviously he had been well advised and well briefed. But underneath it all there was a radical streak of thought which was all his own. When King, he might well surprise us. The present state of the nation – our industry decaying, our social services being destroyed – must anger him greatly.

13

The National Steel Strike

British Steel's demand that we lose a further 10,000 jobs and receive a 'modest' national increase, which would in no way compensate for the 17.4 per cent rise in inflation, put us on a headlong course to conflict. Other groups of workers had settled for what now seems an incredible average of 16 per cent that year. The key negotiating meeting with BSC was held on 3 December 1979 at Grosvenor Place.

Fifty delegates and our full-time officers listened to Bob Scholey and his team tell us what was on offer: precisely nothing. BSC, the chief executive declared again, was not prepared to make any new money available nationally. All it would promise was to honour a commitment made the previous year to consolidate into basic rates 2 per cent of the money already awarded to us.

A zero increase did not go down too well with the delegates, and their wrath was not lessened when BSC added that we could have local productivity deals which might raise as much as 4 per cent in some areas, although that 4 per cent had to be self-financing. In other words, cuts would have to be made, and most of these savings would come about by men and women walking out of the works gate for good. This was the first time we had ever been made this kind of offer; the Corporation was obviously trying to change the whole process of pay negotiations. Feelings within my delegation ran very high.

We continued to press strongly for a change in the attitude of the Corporation, but to no avail. Even so, the meeting was still reasonably quiet – we were biting our tongues. In view of the futility of further argument, I asked for an adjournment; this lasted for a considerable period of time while our delegation showed their dissatisfaction with the management's offer and attitude in no uncertain terms. We were faced with the desire for action to be taken in the event of no offer being forthcoming; most of the delegates wanted an opportunity to express to management the anger they felt. 'After all the agonies we've gone through, all the cutbacks, all the tightening up, the increase in productivity, and they kick us in the teeth,' one of our people declared.

When we resumed, I explained that one or two of our delegates wished to put their viewpoint directly to Bob Scholey and his colleagues. One by one the steelworkers put their case. The meeting remained orderly until the abrasive, testy director of Teesside Division, Derek Saul, intervened on the management side and said he was disgusted to hear the steelworkers repeating their case 'in dialect after dialect'. This created a near riot; our feelings were summed up by Bill Irvine of the Ravenscraig works, an Executive Council member, who jumped up, angry and quivering with emotion. He glared at Bob Scholey and an astonished Derek Saul (who had embarrassed even his own team). Bill shouted, 'You can keep your 2 per cent and stick it up your f— arse.' The meeting dissolved into chaos, and we adjourned.

In a private session, our delegates told me they were livid. I was instructed to inform BSC that in the event of our not receiving any offer from the Corporation, we would request our Executive Council to embark upon strike action in support of our claim.

On the same day that we were involved in these critical negotiations a delegation of the National Union of Blastfurnacemen were also due to meet the Corporation in the same building. During one of our adjournments we informed them of what had transpired in our meeting and told them that it was our intention to recommend strike action to our Executive Council. They took the same view. The offer made to them was also totally unacceptable and they would take the same lines as the ISTC.

As a result of our failure to reach agreement with BSC I called a special meeting of my full Executive Council on Friday, 7 December, at 4 p.m. and the Corporation's 'offer' of the 2 per cent consolidation, zero national pay increase and up to 4 per cent locally agreed self-financing deals. By now telegrams demanding strike action and promising support had begun to flow in from almost every area in the country. The Executive finally decided to call an official strike of our BSC members. The strike would start at midnight on 2 January 1980. It was not going to be a happy Christmas for any of us.

The Executive Council, on my recommendation, decided that our members in the private sector of the steel industry (about 20 per cent of the industry) would not be called on to strike as they were not directly involved, but they would be instructed not to work on any BSC orders or to do anything that would affect the strike. BSC was given approximately three weeks' notice of the strike and, while some might criticize this delay, we were, and are, a union of high principles and wanted to allow the industry, the Corporation and the government breathing space to reflect and then resolve the situation.

We duly informed the TUC of our decision and at a meeting at Congress House, in London, attended by the general secretaries of all the unions in steel, there was general agreement that the offer BSC had made was completely unrealistic and unacceptable. It was eventually agreed that we should seek an urgent meeting with the chairman of BSC, Sir Charles Villiers, to impress upon him the serious consequences that could result from the failure of the Corporation to make a reasonable offer. Sir Charles was also informed that, unless this was done, all steel unions would recommend to their executives support of the Iron and Steel Trades Confederation.

Later that day we held an Executive Council meeting and I reported the TUC discussion. The Executive decided to give dispensation to certain BSC operations which were not affected by the negotiations: Dowlais, Cleckheaton, Middlesbrough Constructional, Darlington and Simpson and Distington. The Executive unanimously reaffirmed its previous decision to withdraw labour from BSC on 2 January.

My greatest worry was whether the other unions which had promised 'support' in the event of BSC refusing to improve its offer would come out with us, or whether we would have to stand alone. Hector Smith, general secretary of the National Union of Blastfurnacemen, asked if the executives of both unions could meet. They were with us. The blastfurnacemen at least would definitely be on strike too.

On Sunday, 30 December, two days before the strike was due to begin, Woodrow Wyatt, who was then writing a column in the *Sunday Mirror*, told readers that the steel strike was 'sheer suicide'. His criticisms of us were so outrageously wrong that I wrote to him and presented our case. He got in touch and we met. He listened carefully to what I had to say and, in the next issue of the *Sunday Mirror*, completely retracted everything he had said the previous week. He blamed the British Steel Corporation for its intransigence, and thereafter he gave us a lot of help. He had contacts with the Prime Minister and the British Steel Corporation, and arranged for facilities so that meetings could be held away from the press on a number of occasions. At all times he was trying to help us gain a satisfactory settlement.

The strike, to the surprise of the government, the civil service, the media and the public (but not to those who knew us) was 100 per cent successful. Every single member of the ISTC supported it (a situation Britain's miners must have envied during their own dispute). Not a works was in operation, not a mill moved. Only the furnaces flickered because we had to keep them secure and safe ready for when we resumed operations.

Two days after the strike began a delegation comprising Len Murray, Moss Evans, David Basnett, Hector Smith and I met representatives of British Steel led by Bob Scholey – or 'Black Bob' as he was known with increasing venom. After a long discussion the Corporation increased its offer from 2 per cent consolidation plus 4 per cent local deals to 2 per cent plus 6 per cent. There was a little more to be had, it seemed, from the local productivity deals or 'lump-sum bonus schemes' as they were known.

In an attempt to make further progress we asked if Sir Charles Villiers the chairman of BSC, could attend the meeting and after a while he came into the room. He listened to the arguments for a while, and it was then that we saw evidence of the friction that existed between him and Bob Scholey. At one point Sir Charles intervened, and it seemed to us that what he was saying was that he would like to consider further the proposals we were making. Suddenly Bob Scholey got to his feet and walked out – indicating his dissatisfaction at Sir Charles's intervention. This departure created a rather uncomfortable feeling and there was a lot of shuffling of feet. The incident highlighted one of the difficulties we were to have. There had been stories of rifts between Sir Charles and Bob Scholey and now it seemed quite clear that they were at loggerheads.

Because of this difficult situation we decided as a negotiating group to seek a meeting with the BSC board. They would have to have the final say on the Corporation's behalf. But would they meet us? I was not optimistic. Not once since the steel industry had been nationalized had the Corporation's board of directors met representatives of the workforce. If a new Labour Government brings back into the public domain major industries which have in whole or in part been privatized, then I hope they will give a great deal of thought to the structures of these enterprises. I hope there will be worker directors with real power to direct the enterprise.

I wrote to every member of the board giving them a full statement of our case on a number of issues relating to investment, closure and redundancies and the commercial aspects of the industry, and I sought a meeting with them. However, as I expected, they refused to meet us. I wrote again. Did they not realize that in refusing to meet us they were doing nothing more than acting as rubber stamps for the decisions of the chairman and chief executive?

The other unions in steel were more shocked than we

were by the board's refusal to meet. We had anticipated it. Moss Evans was particularly angry. On 4 January the TGWU announced that it was officially joining the ISTC and the Blastfurnacemen, and all its members were being recommended to join the strike, if they had not already withdrawn their labour. Within thirty-six hours the board had agreed to meet us.

The TUC Coordinating Committee, as our negotiating group became known, met the board on 7 January. The board said they would confirm the 2 per cent consolidation, give a 6 per cent national increase and confirmed that up to 6 per cent would be available from local deals. But – and this was the big but – there were some far-reaching conditions. There had to be agreements on more changes in working practices, further redundancies, reduced manning and a total block on the recruitment of labour. The whole agreement had to be self-financing. And local productivity deals had to be signed by 31 March that year. All this proved too much, and the Coordinating Committee made it clear it was unacceptable.

From then on, the executives of the ISTC and the Blastfurnacemen met regularly together. We became firm friends and trusted colleagues. We decided that we would meet to discuss what we should do about the private sector which was still at work, and so prior to the meeting on 16 January I met ISTC delegations from the various private sector negotiating panels. The delegates pleaded that they should not become involved. A number of their works were making losses or only breaking even. They feared they might go under. I agreed with them and promised to put their case. Happily, the two executives accepted what I had to say, provided the private firms refused to handle BSC orders.

The craftsmen within our industry – those represented by the AUEW, the EEPTU and other smaller unions – were under instructions from their officials to pass through the picket lines. Although many craftsmen had in fact come out with us, this was an embarrassing situation and could not last for long. The craft unions met under the umbrella of the National Craftsmen's Coordinating Committee and officials of that committee came under considerable pressure from their members who wanted all the craft unions to declare the strike official. On 9 January, the committee had to act, and it recommended to each individual union Executive that the strike should be made official. It also decided to join with the Transport and General Workers Union and the General and Municipal Workers Union, giving them just under half the trade union members in the industry, and continue with separate negotiations with the British Steel Corporation, as was the custom.

On 16 January I wrote to the Prime Minister seeking a meeting so that Hector Smith and I could put to her our proposals for settlement of the strike and to seek her assistance. The Prime Minister replied that she would be very ready to see us. She asked us to first meet the Secretary of State for Industry and the Secretary of State for Employment, and explained that at the same time she would have to extend the same courtesy to Sir Charles Villiers and Bob Scholey. The Prime Minister added that, contrary to press reports, she had not discussed the strike with the BSC management.

Hector Smith and I accompanied by Sandy Feather, national staff officer of the ISTC, met the Prime Minister on 21 January at 10 Downing Street. At the meeting were Jim Prior, Secretary of State for Employment, and Sir Keith Joseph, Secretary of State for Industry.

The Prime Minister was dressed in a very neat green outfit which looked quite smart. She shook hands with us on being introduced by Jim Prior. We sat on easy chairs in a comfortable lounge in 10 Downing Street with Mrs Thatcher facing us.

Mrs Thatcher was very keen to show an interest in the problems that we were experiencing and at the same time to outline her political approach on the economic front. Whilst she was reasonably well briefed on the industry she seemed a little apprehensive on occasions and kept turning to Sir Keith Joseph to ask for confirmation of points that she was raising. But I was rather surprised when I reminded her that the Consett works had been condemned to total closure. She said, 'Surely not,' and once again turned to Jim Prior and Sir Keith Joseph, who confirmed that this was correct. Mrs Thatcher was leaning forward on her chair in her eagerness to persuade us of the difficulties being faced by government. We were courteously treated, but at that stage we had our suspicions that the government had intervened behind the scenes from day one of the strike to prevent payments being made to steelworkers. Thus workers in the steel industry were singled out for no increase whatsoever.

During the meeting we were served tea and, most amusingly, Sir Keith Joseph was provided with a pot of honey instead of sugar for his tea. We may live in a land of milk and honey, but on this occasion we were there for the money and in the hope that they would give consideration to our plea.

A short time later I received a request from the Conservative Parliamentary Employment Committee to speak to them, which I did on 23 January at the House of Commons. It was an extremely good meeting, at which only one out of about sixty members was openly hostile and critical. As for the rest, they seemed to be reflecting on the seriousness of the situation and on the points I was making.

Whether the discussion with the Prime Minister had any impact or not I will never know, but the Secretary of State for Industry had said beforehand that there would be no more funds for wage increases for steelworkers. In the event, we did win more, and I would like to think that our meeting with Mrs Thatcher had some slight impact.

The strike took on an international complexion when we were visited by Herman Rebhan, general secretary of the International Metalworkers Federation, who was accompanied by representatives from fifteen countries. They had come to pledge international support, and Mr Rebhan – a vigorous, lively minded American whom I came to admire greatly – promised to put our case to the Federation and gave us financial assistance, which was very helpful. But in addition they contacted all our colleagues in metal unions in the rest of the world asking for support. I G Metall of Germany donated approximately £60,000 towards our strike costs and other unions helped to a much lesser degree. The British T U C collected something in the region of £60,000. However, this was only a drop in the ocean as our strike costs were in the region of £2½ million.

Sid Weighell, general secretary of the National Union of Railwaymen, was the first man to indicate that his union would be prepared to do all possible to help us in our struggle. I later met the Executive of the train drivers union, A S L E F, which committed itself to full support. Although we had received indications of support from the dockers, the seamen and the Transport and General Workers Union, we were faced with one big problem. Steel imports were still coming into Britain and lorry drivers were still ferrying these consignments around. Because of the continued import of steel things began to get tough.

Most of the private-sector members of our Executive still felt they should not be involved in the dispute, but others began taking the view that if they were instructed to join the strike they would loyally obey the call from the Executive. At another meeting of our Executive, despite my further plea that the private sector be kept out and be used as a bargaining counter to put pressure on the government, the Executive took the decision that our members in the private sector would be called out on strike on Sunday, 27 January.

The decision to involve the private sector further was bound to have ramifications. Many of the works concerned were running into severe financial difficulties as the effects of the strike compounded earlier problems. There were difficulties at Sheerness where our members flatly refused to accept the instruction of the Executive and come out. We also had problems at Hadfields in Sheffield where there was mass picketing, albeit in a reasonable and peaceful manner, in an attempt to keep our members from going into work. I even had a visit from a busload of representatives from Hadfields and the chairman, Dan Norton, who came to ask for dispensation. Dispensation meant that we would allow his company to operate without being picketed as it was not involved in the strike. He explained that the plant was in a bad way; if they could not service their customers the possibility was that, ultimately, they would be closed. I recognized that this plant, which is an old, inefficient type of works, would not survive for long under the present circumstances and agreed to give dispensation. A delighted Dan actually offered me £25,000 towards our strike fund – which I thought was a very generous gesture – but I could not accept it, as it could have been looked upon as an act of bribery. The Strike Committee in the Sheffield Area, however, saw things totally differently and refused to accept the dispensation.

Tiny Rowland of Lonrho came into the act when he sought a meeting with Sir Charles Villiers in an attempt to persuade him to improve the Corporation's offer and secure an end to what was becoming a very damaging strike. He apparently was not very impressed by what he found at Grosvenor Place, particularly the performance of Sir Charles Villiers and his colleagues.

The next challenge that we faced came from the courts. After our decision to involve the private sector the Independent Steel Employers took legal action. I reported to a special meeting of my Executive on 24 January that I had received a letter from the chairman of the British Independent Steel Producers Association telling me that sixteen companies subscribing to the Association had decided to take out a writ in the High Court, together with a restraining injunction, to prevent members of the private sector from being involved in the BSC dispute. On 25 January the application for the injunction was heard and refused by Judge Kenneth Jones, who held that, arising from rulings of the House of Lords in the case of *McShane* v. *The Express Newspapers*, the union had done no legal wrong. The judge finished giving his judgment just before 5 p.m., by which time all the court clerks and judges have usually left for home. However, at 5.30 p.m. our solicitors were told that the Court of Appeal was being convened to sit the following morning under the chairmanship of Lord Denning to hear the employers' appeal. Our legal advisers did not know of any previous case in which the courts had been so co-operative in hearing cases at such short notice.

The night before Lord Denning was due to give judgment I visited Scunthorpe to see the stockpiling of millions of tonnes of imported steel. I was very worried about the result of the appeal. I was certain that Lord Denning would overturn the judgment of Justice Kenneth Jones; were we once again to experience Lord Denning's brand of 'justice' in which the decisions of other judges were completely ignored? I slept very little that night. Next day, as expected, Lord Denning reversed the decision.

On Sunday I called together union officials and our solicitors and we decided to approach the House of Lords for a reversal of Lord Denning's judgment. This time it was we who were successful in obtaining a hearing at extremely short notice. We made our approach on the Monday and the House of Lords was due to sit on the following Friday.

Before the hearing two things happened that I shall never forget. First, I attended a rally in Cardiff which was arranged to protest against government job cuts. All TUC unions were present, but the vast majority of the workers on the march were steelworkers. At the rally itself, which was held in Sophia Gardens and was attended by Michael Foot and other prominent Welsh politicians and trade union leaders, there was standing room only. A number of speakers made contributions and then, when the chairman finally announced my name and I rose to speak, the whole building erupted in a tremendous crescendo of sound, all delegates shouting 'We want Bill!' It was the most moving experience I have ever known and I could not prevent the tears of emotion rolling down my cheeks. My wife, who was at the other end of the platform, cried too. I cannot remember much of what I said that day, other than that if the judgment of Denning meant a refusal by my Executive Council to obey the law, I would accept that decision even if this meant my going to prison. On that day I would have died for the people who stood and cheered and cried with me.

The second drama came on 29 January when my Executive met to decide whether to comply with Lord Denning's judgment. I informed the Executive that by going to the House of Lords we would have an opportunity for the position to be examined on behalf of the whole trade union movement. After all, we would all be affected by the decision. I pointed out that our organization had conscientiously followed the law of the land up to the present time, and that we should continue to do so. Any mass protest might embarrass our legal advisers handling the appeal at the House of Lords, and the hearing should take place without impediment. After a long and difficult meeting I succeeded in getting the majority of the Executive to accept my recommendations. Even Mrs Thatcher later acknowledged the constructive approach of the ISTC.

What followed is now legal history. The Law Lords met on Friday, 1 February, and very quickly pronounced judgment reversing Lord Denning's decision. They gave the unions the right to involve the private sector again.

At a meeting of the joint executives of the ISTC and NUB that day it was resolved that as from Sunday, 3 February, an instruction would be given to all our private sector members that they should withdraw their labour. Once again I was faced with a decision which I felt was not helpful to the cause of the strike. The controversy would avert from the public eye the strong arguments that we had against BSC; instead the spotlight would be thrown on the private sector, which would be regarded as the innocent victim of the dispute. I think the last straw so far as the ISTC Executive was concerned was that we had proof that some of the private sector employers were actually helping BSC by taking on their customers and by accepting material belonging to BSC for distribution. That was something which could not be defended and it played a big part in the decision to try to shut all steel plants.

One thing that pleased me a great deal was that we were winning the propaganda war; indeed, *The Times* later ran an article pointing out how well we had presented our case to the public through the media and how dismally British Steel was performing.

The first thing I did when I knew we were plunging headlong into conflict was to confer with two industrial editors of national newspapers which were sympathetic to our cause and with Keith Bill, who was head of publications at British Steel and was to become my press adviser. We discussed our approach to the press, how we would present ourselves and what the main themes should be. We decided on a policy of answering every question, telling the truth (although sometimes resorting to the traditional plea of 'that's off the record') and giving journalists as many details and as much background information as possible any time of the day or night. If things became difficult we took the initiative. For example, on one occasion the *Sun* ran a very bitter editorial against us. I rang the editor, Larry Lamb and asked if I could meet him. I went to his office early in the evening for a meeting that was to last 'a few minutes'. In the event I stayed for an hour arguing our case. He agreed to give us space to put our point of view. We had over half a page to write exactly what we wanted.

Our positive attitude towards the press paid off. The complaints we had about media coverage were very few indeed. In fact, when the strike was over I thanked all the hard-working journalists who had helped us so much. The journalists for their part were happy with the way they had been treated. After the strike they gave me and a number of my officers a wonderful 'thank you' dinner and night out at Ronnie Scott's Jazz Club.

Within the trade union movement it is common practice to condemn the press most viciously. They always get the blame for any bad publicity the unions receive and union leaders have been heard criticizing working journalists in shrill, hysterical tones. It is often forgotten that industrial correspondents who cover trade union activities are usually trade unionists themselves and are not responsible for the critical comments that are made in the hostile sections of the press. Although it is true that the trade union move- ment receives a lot of bad publicity, quite often our own attitude towards the press brings out the worst in editors when it comes to critical comment.

At the TUC Congress in 1980, after a number of delegates had fiercely criticized the journalists, we reached the part of the agenda when the general secretary of the TUC thanks the media for their attendance. Traditionally, one of the industrial correspondents replies. At the 1980 Congress, Martin Adeney, industrial editor of BBC Television News, replied on behalf of the media. He was aware that some of his colleagues were smarting at what they thought was unfair criticism that had been made that week, and made a point of saying that we had seen, in the steel strike, the biggest industrial dispute since 1926, and yet there were no complaints from ISTC about press coverage. He said that ISTC had won over public opinion and that the trade union movement would get a better press if it adopted a similar approach to the one we had used.

During the strike something happened in the media which was to shake BSC and the government. The Granada programme 'World in Action' obtained secret top-level papers from BSC. These papers showed that management originally planned a 10½-14 per cent pay offer and that the zero pay award came about as a result of government interference. In other words, the BSC executive was the puppet of the government and the steel strike need never have taken place. The papers also showed direct government involvement during the closing months of 1979. It was only after the strike had begun and the government realized what it had done that the Industry Minister Sir Keith Joseph told BSC it could give the workers more money. It was a complete U-turn.

These revelations were very damaging to the British Steel Corporation which took out an injunction against Granada. At the same time the Corporation set up an investigation to find the mole who had released the papers to Granada. The inquiry went on for many months before the mole was finally tracked down. To the surprise of the British Steel

Corporation it was not a member of the ISTC but a person who had no links whatsoever with the trade unions. He was simply a BSC employee in charge of document processing who thought that he should expose the lies and distortions plainly revealed in the papers.

Hector Smith and I were becoming anxious to resume negotiations with British Steel. At least we should be talking together. We had a chance to sound out Bob Scholey when he and Dr David Grieves, BSC's head of personnel, attended a meeting of the European Coal and Steel Community Consultative Committee in Luxembourg. The government knew the risks but did not believe that the steelworkers would strike. The union had not taken strike action since 1926. During the meeting, Grieves and I found a form of wording about the local productivity schemes that would allow talks to begin again.

Sir Charles Villiers, in discussing the proposals the Corporation were prepared to make, had called them a 'many-splendoured thing'. When the new talks broke down, however, we changed his phraseology to 'many-splendoured sting'. We were still in a position of stalemate, not having advanced as we had hoped.

The difference between us which prevented the continuation of negotiations was the Corporation's insistence that productivity payments should be paid as a quarterly lump sum, but only after we had accepted flexibility, interchangeability, redundancy, reduced manning and privatization. In the discussions at Luxembourg I had understood that we were to receive a 4 per cent payment on entering into productivity talks, and that this payment would be based on the hourly or shift rate and paid on the signing of the national agreement.

On 10 February we became aware of the reason why the Corporation had changed its mind. They had been meeting privately with the Craftsmen's Co-ordinating Committee and the other unions in that group. Without any discussions with us, the craftsmen's committee had reached an agreement with the Corporation whereby they would receive a 10 per cent increase plus a 4 per cent productivity lump-sum payment. This agreement included all the objectionable features we refused to accept: complete and immediate flexibility, interchangeability and redundancy. It was unfortunate that the leaders of the craft and other unions who had signed the agreement totally misread the feelings of their own members. For when the agreement was taken back to the delegate conferences of the different unions it was overwhelmingly rejected, first by the Transport and General Workers Union, then by the craft and other unions, leaving their negotiating team completely isolated and without any credibility. So we were still at stalemate and from then on I was suspicious of the activities of a few of the craft union leaders.

Things were not helped by the announcement that Sir Charles Villiers' own salary was to be increased by 16·3 per cent in April (without strings) and that this followed a hitherto unpublicized rise of 32·8 per cent (without strings) the previous year. You can imagine the feelings of the striking steelworkers who were being offered nothing at all.

We met the Corporation again a little later but this meeting too ended in disarray. It was very disappointing to the trade union side, particularly as on two occasions Bob Scholey had privately mentioned to a few of us the possibility of going as far as 14 per cent but no further. Yet on the resumption of negotiations BSC were not even offering a 13 per cent increase on the weekly pay packet.

This breakdown was followed by an inconclusive meeting with ACAS (Advisory Conciliation and Arbitration Service) – and another call from Woodrow Wyatt, who expressed his great disappointment at the failure of the talks. He had been in constant touch with me over a long period of time, and also with the Prime Minister and British Steel, and in his private discussions he was of the opinion that 8 per cent plus a 5 per cent productivity payment would seem a reasonable proposal for the resumption of negotiations.

Jim Callaghan, Leader of the Opposition, called me at my home a few days later. He wanted to know the exact state of affairs, and I agreed that Hector Smith and I should meet him. I also discussed the matter with Solly Gross, first secretary at the Department of Trade and Industry, who was trying to persuade us to refer the matter to arbitration in the hope of an early settlement. Both Jim Callaghan and Solly Gross agreed that, following the abortive attempt of the craft and other unions to make an agreement, it was now up to the ISTC and the Blastfurnacemen to find a way out of the impasse.

Later, in Paris at a conference of the Organization for Economic Cooperation and Development to discuss the steel crisis throughout the Western industralized world, I again met Solly Gross. I was there to present the International Metalworkers Federation's case for an international plan for steel that would help prevent the continued erosion of jobs. We were looking for orderly marketing and cooperation within the steel industry throughout the world. The conference gave me the chance to raise again the strike issue with Solly Gross, who is a very sincere man and a keen advocate for the steel industry. As we were talking, Gavin Laird, now AEUW general secretary, joined us. We discussed a new proposal I had put to Solly Gross which might enable us to get back to negotiations. Within less than a week, however, I was informed by Solly that he had received a severe reprimand from his superiors and told not to interfere with the negotiations. Knowing the need for confidentiality, I had not spoken to anyone about my talk with Solly. It was therefore a most disagreeable surprise that his involvement through our discussions became known within the Department of Trade and Industry.

Still more private sector chiefs beat a path to my door, this time Swarj Paul of National Gas Tubes and Maurice Webb of Alpha Steel. These were not easy discussions because both men are excellent private employers who fully support trade unions at their works. But I was unable to give them any hopeful news.

Then came another invitation to more talks with BSC, this time at a secret venue. I was accompanied by Hector Smith, my own president Les Bramley, and Nick Leadley, president of the NUB. We were informed, while staying at the Dragonara Hotel in Middlesbrough, that the meeting would be held at the Airport Hotel, Teesside. We wanted to get there without the press, but the reporters were not going to have that and followed us in a convoy of cars. 'Put your foot down, Ken,' I told Ken Clarke, ISTC national officer. 'Let's lose them.' Ken took off at high speed round the country lanes with the journalists in pursuit. When we arrived, one car screeched up behind us and out staggered Giles Smith, ITN industrial editor, whose nerves, he said, were 'shattered'.

BSC's representatives had beaten the press by flying up from London by private jet and going straight to the airport conference room. We had a three-hour meeting, but all BSC tried to do was to press on us the same discredited agreement accepted by the craft and other union leaders but decisively rejected by their members.

The following day I attended a demonstration march and rally in Motherwell city centre. Thousands were there, morale was good, and after seven weeks on strike no one was complaining about the lack of money (we paid no strike pay; had we done so we would have run out of cash and used up our £11 million assets within a very short space of time), or demanding to go back to work. We were still absolutely solid.

As the strike wore on, every day brought another problem. I was extremely worried about a massive demonstration there was to be outside a private company, Sheerness Steel, in Kent; I was concerned about the possibility of losing public sympathy with such a large demonstration. I had been assured by my colleagues that the event would be well stewarded and peaceful, and so it proved – although our members were abused, spat on and refused service in local shops and pubs. We failed to persuade our colleagues at Sheerness not to go back to work, but at least we did not sacrifice public sympathy.

Another problem hit us on 27 February. Our Rotherham office was sabotaged by someone who set fire to the building. A member of our strike committee, Bruce Wooton, was on duty alone in the office, which was on the first floor, when he heard a loud explosion. He was unable to use the staircase to escape from the building because of the smoke and flames. He telephoned the fire brigade, then jumped from a first-floor window at the front of the building, suffering a broken ankle and bruises. The police and forensic experts carried out a full investigation, and concluded that the fire was caused by someone entering the building through the rear door and pouring five gallons of petrol on the floor. This was then ignited through the main door letter box. The ensuing explosion must have frightened even the arsonist. There was extensive damage to the building, estimated at around £50,000.

It is not unusual during long strikes like ours for the union and the union leader to be the target of threatening letters and criticism. I received a number of death threats which I regarded as being the work of cranks. Nevertheless, one is obliged to hand these letters to the police who may wish to follow them up. I naturally kept all knowledge of such threats from my wife and family, but unfortunately on one occasion someone sent a letter to my local sports centre which in turn forwarded it to my home. Joan read it – and it took me a long time to reassure her. I received lots of insulting letters, but many more of support.

Our union also suffered other attacks, including a picket cabin being burned to the ground. But the police were unable to find the culprits of any of the attacks upon us.

I abhor violence of any sort and I think that had I been an executive member of the NUM during their dispute I would have hung my head in shame. By their silence they set the union movement back twenty years. They also put labour leader Neil Kinnock in a very difficult position. He could have presented the miners' case very effectively, but he could not afford to be too closely identified with them in the public mind – and that was the fault of the NUM Executive. And some of them had the cheek to criticize him!

The strike dragged on, and Len Murray contacted Hector Smith and me during the first week of March. The craft unions, he said, felt left out of things since their abortive attempt to get an agreement. Could they join us in our endeavours to achieve an end to the dispute? We accepted this, and on 4 March two delegates each from my own union, the NUB, the TGWU, General and Municipal Workers and the Electricians representing the Craftsmen met at the TUC's Congress House in London.

After a fairly lengthy discussion we agreed to set up a coordination committee for further talks with BSC. To strengthen our hand, Moss Evans instructed all members of his huge union to observe all our picket lines. We had been seeking to persuade lorry drivers not to transport steel for nine weeks; at last the TGWU was to act!

Then BSC went on the attack, announcing a ballot of the workforce, to be conducted over our heads. The ballot was not well organized; some members received two ballot forms, forms were circulated to dozens of steelworkers who had retired or had died, and extra forms were handed out to any employees who claimed they had mislaid or lost their forms. We registered a protest about these infringements with the Electoral Reform Society which lost credibility refusing to investigate the circumstances. The result of the ballot showed that 56 per cent of employees had either voted against the Corporation or refused to vote. We had advised our branches not to participate in the ballot.

The determination of steelworkers to win the dispute was clearly demonstrated at a consultation conference of delegates from all the steel unions. There was absolutely no sign that anyone wanted to give in. The following day I had an interesting confrontation with Sir Charles Villiers on the 'TV Eye' programme. Throughout the strike I had set time aside each day for the media – especially for radio, which our strikers tuned to – but this television programme with Sir Charles Villiers was our first public confrontation.

We both put our points of view, and the one thing that came across was that Sir Charles did not have the stomach for the fight. I recalled a comment he made to one of my colleagues who visited him at his home a week before the strike began. 'It's Bob Scholey, of course,' he said, 'he's the hawk and I'm the dove.' If only we could bring him back into the negotiating arena!

On 10 March it was back to ACAS to see director of ACAS Jim Mortimer and then off to see BSC with the new united co-ordinating group of union leaders. The talks were to go on for three days, and as session followed session and presentation followed presentation we moved towards an agreement on a 14 per cent increase plus a 5 per cent local productivity payment. Then, suddenly and surprisingly, it was all off. The talks broke down. We felt badly let down, as it appeared the Corporation had been leading us along blind paths and that they did not intend to make an agreement. We seemed to be getting nowhere slowly.

I think some of the frustration I felt came out in a 'Jimmy Young Show' interview a couple of days later. It was now almost becoming a war of nerves and I told listeners that I was now despairing that the government and BSC wanted an agreement at all. I do not think anyone, unless they have experienced it, can appreciate the tensions, the wearying ceaseless pressures of leading a great national strike. You are out there with your colleagues, but at the same time very much on your own. You have to find a way forward, and all the time you know your members, indeed the industry, are suffering.

I was asked afterwards how I kept sane. First, I played squash whenever I could, often with *Guardian* labour editor Keith Harper; then I ran, as I have done most of my life – usually six miles each morning; and I prayed. When you are the leader of a union in a big industrial dispute, who else is there that you can turn to but Him? I had always, as a boy, enjoyed the singing in the Salvation Army halls, but it took a national strike to bring me closer to an understanding of a loving God.

On 18 March the executives of the Blastfurnacemen and ISTC took the crucial decision of seeking third-party intervention through a Court of Inquiry. Two days later the trade union Coordinating Committee agreed to seek one further meeting with BSC and inform them that we intended to ask for a Committee of Inquiry if these talks failed.

We met the Corporation but there was no further progress, so I followed the Coordinating Committee's wishes and sought a meeting with Industry Minister Jim Prior. Mr Prior said that the government did not wish to intervene except through the medium of ACAS, and he had no intention of setting up an official Court of Inquiry. His one helpful suggestion was that we set up a Committee of Inquiry between the British Steel Corporation and ourselves.

Later the same day when I returned to my office I found telegrams from the Rotherham and Scottish strike committees requesting that there should be no return to work. There was also the possibility that the dock strike which had started in Liverpool would spread to other docks in support of the steelworkers. For eleven weeks dockers had been unloading millions of tonnes of imported steel, and now at last they wanted to join in!

Over the period of 21 to 23 March I had a number of phone calls from Woodrow Wyatt, who was seeking to give further assistance and wished to know the exact position of the trade unions in relation to the dispute. On the Sunday he made proposals regarding interim payments from the Corporation on the understanding that, following the setting up of a Committee of Inquiry, our people would return to work. I said we would have to see.

On 25 March BSC and the Coordinating Committee met and it was agreed that we set up a Committee of Inquiry and that ACAS would be involved in making the arrangements. The British Steel Corporation had, as Woodrow Wyatt predicted, indicated that if we returned to work after the setting up of the Committee of Inquiry they would be prepared to make an interim payment to all employees of 10 per cent. This was rejected by the executives of the Blastfurnacemen and ISTC which would not consider a request for a return to work while the inquiry was going on. The reason for this was that the Corporation had refused to accept that the Committee of Inquiry should examine not only the dispute on pay but the management of British Steel itself.

Names were being suggested by various people for the

chairmanship of the committee, and we agreed to accept Harold Lever, former Labour Cabinet Minister. We on the trade union side then asked Bill Keys, general secretary of SOGAT (Society for Graphical and Allied Trades), to act on our behalf, and the employers' representative was Sir Richard Marsh, the former Labour Minister and now a peer.

Then we had yet another crisis: the other unions which earlier in the dispute had conducted their own separate negotiations (leading to the eventual agreement being over-turned by their own members), decided once more to go it alone. At the Committee of Inquiry the workforce was to be represented by two groups. There still seemed to be a lot of jealousy around, but I decided to make no comment and to let events take their course.

But friction and acrimony grew between the two groups of unions, the ISTC and the NUB on the one hand and the rest on the other, and things were not improved when Gavin Laird of the AUEW said at the outset of the inquiry that, regardless of the decision of the committee his group would recommend to their members that they accept it and go back to work. I could not understand this at all. To achieve the Committee of Inquiry, we had worked together as a trade union Coordinating Committee. Now, here was the leader of one group making disruptive public statements without any consultation. Tactically, the NCCC's comments weakened our position. If they were saying that their unions would accept absolutely any decision of the committee, then there was no pressure on the members of that committee to come up with something that would be acceptable to both sides.

The final recommendation of the committee was this: an 11 per cent increase across the board, plus 4 per cent from local productivity, plus other bits and pieces – overall, an increase of 15.95 per cent.

That was an offer that our Executive might well accept. From zero national pay award to 15·95 per cent was a fine win, well worth fighting for. The employers had tried to rub the steelworkers' noses in the dust. Perhaps, as many of us suspected, and as the Granada 'steel papers' appeared to show, the government was actually using the BSC board to force a showdown and to prove to all British workers how tough they were. After all the sacrifices the steelworkers had made, the employers' 'zero increase offer' was seen as a personal insult. That is why, to the last worker, they rose up in revolt.

I could not help but reflect, however, that if we had had one single union for the whole of the steel industry, how much stronger our position would have been. Had we all been pulling together as a team in a tug-of-war, things might have been different. One of the TUC's great disappointments was in not making further progress towards a single union for each industry. Perhaps the day will come when in each industry in Britain, be it steel or the railways, computers or catering, there is only one union for the employers to negotiate with and only one union to which the government need speak. This is the pattern our continental competitors have successfully adopted, and it has proved of great benefit to the workforce.

Most steelworkers hailed the Committee of Inquiry award as a clear vindication of their action, but others felt we had failed by not getting 20 per cent – the slogan Arthur Scargill had introduced into our strike vocabulary. On 1 April, I formally reported back to the negotiating committees of the production unions, the NUB and ourselves, and the Committee of Inquiry's recommendation was accepted by forty-two votes to twenty-seven. Then the NUB and ISTC executives met separately to ratify the decision. My own Executive meeting was lengthy and quite abrasive. There were more wanting to reach the magical 20 per cent than I had thought. But the Blastfurnacemen, who had been meeting in another room, sent a message to say they were fed up with waiting and wanted to join us immediately – or they would go home! They came in – and within two hours both executives had endorsed the decision of the negotiating committees and decided that there should be a return to work within BSC on Thursday, 3 April, at 6 a.m.

After making this decision we allowed a group of forty

pickets who had come into our Swinton House headquarters in Gray's Inn Road to come into the meeting to make their points. It was an angry scene – they wanted that 20 per cent! There was a lot of verbal abuse, and two of the pickets threw their union cards at me. 'You can stick your union!' they shouted. 'We're off!' When I picked up the torn cards afterwards I found the pickets were both members of the TGWU! I was happy to send them on to Moss Evans.

In the end the pickets departed and I was left to deal with the final press conference. Aftwards, while I was being interviewed for television, three young pickets barged in. They said they had been party to the agitation in our council chamber earlier and had been thinking. They wished to apologize for their behaviour and also congratulated me on the job I had done.

The appreciation of ordinary members meant a great deal to me, as did the support of my own family. The relationship between Joan and me and our two children is extremely good and we are particularly close. My daughter has two children, Joanne and Victoria, who are now young ladies. Joanne lives with us and is working for her A-levels at school, whilst Victoria is living with her parents in Sydney, Australia. My son John, a solicitor, is married and has a delightful baby daughter, Rebecca Jane. The warmth and love of them all has meant much to me.

I often look back and smile at the amusing incidents during the dispute. One reporter, who worked for Sir James Goldsmith's magazine *Now!*, visited us so often that he began answering the phones, which never stopped ringing. In the end he was so busy he virtually became an honorary strike coordinator! I often wondered what Sir James would think if he knew – and I marvelled how an Eton education, which the reporter had enjoyed, could fit one so well for something other than a job in the City or the Palace of Westminster!

Throughout the period of the strike I was in constant touch not only with my national officials and regional officers, but also with the lay officers and the ordinary members of the ISTC who were mounting picket lines on every dock in the country, on several stockholders and on other steel works. It was warming to find that everywhere both male and female members were extremely active in providing sandwiches, soup and so on on a community basis for all our members involved in strike activities.

Whilst it is true that people suffer great hardship during a strike, it is also a fact that there is a rekindling of the community spirit that used to exist many years ago and a willingness to help one another out; people used to the last ounce all the goods and food they could afford, and were also prepared to put into the central pool money and food to make sure that no one would starve during this period. We also attempted to persuade local councils and building societies not to press for full repayment of either rent or mortgage during the strike, and I must say that they were very co-operative.

Naturally during such periods of hardship all families spend less on clothing, food and entertainment, but there were certain people who were particularly hard-hit. I recall one lady in the Sheffield area writing to me asking for help. She was single, middle-aged and thus receiving no social security benefit whatsoever. I am afraid that in the appeals that were made it was very difficult to single out any one person who was suffering hardship. I did, however, send this lady a gift of £10 out of my own pocket, because under the rules of the organization she did not qualify for any other payment. There were other single people who received nothing from the state during the strike, and yet the deprivation they suffered was still not sufficient to turn them against the objective of winning the strike.

14

More Successes

After the strike there were a succession of similar works closures or partial closures, and this distressed me greatly. But in almost every case, sometimes despite our pleadings for men and women to stand and fight with us, the promise of redundancy payments was just too tempting.

Steel was going through a worldwide crisis because every developing nation wanted a steel plant and an airline as a sign of its maturity. When things get rough it is easy to ground one or two planes, but it is quite a different matter when you have a multimillion steel works operating twenty-four hours a day. So governments around the globe poured money into their plants to keep them going, and consequently the world was awash with steel.

One of the problems so far as Britain was concerned was that Mrs Thatcher's government, for all the talk of strength and leadership, had no appetite for standing and fighting for Britain if it meant upsetting industrialists in Europe. For some inexplicable reason we had to be gentlemen, ever showing the way. We were the first country to reduce our own steel operations and, worse, we took a much larger share of the cut in Europe than did other EEC states, which must have laughed to themselves as they watched the British Government lead steel to the slaughter. In the event, our 'example' did nothing at all to move the Italians, Belgians and others to cut their capacities to reduce the surplus in Europe. Indeed, the Italians increased output as soon as they saw us withdraw from our markets.

The British Government was also to blame for not putting our costs on the same footing as those of our

European rivals. The cost of our raw materials and energy was considerably higher than those of our competitors simply because we had a government bent on aiding banking, insurance services and tourism at the expense of Britain's traditional industries. Even the CBI joined us in our call for a restructuring of energy tariffs so that big users of electricity, like steel, would have their energy at a cheaper rate while domestic users paid a little more. This was the system every other country in Europe enjoyed. In Britain 40 per cent of the costs of many steel plants goes on energy, so if the government had given us some relief plants could have been saved, and taxpayers' money would not have been wasted on unemployment pay, social security benefits and making up for the shortfall in tax revenues arising from the loss of jobs in the steel industry. One of the greatest criminal follies of all time has been the way that Britain has used every penny of our income from North Sea oil and gas to maintain the dole queue.

There were, however, some successes that we enjoyed after our thirteen-week steel stoppage. The first came when British Steel announced that it wanted to close one of the two big integrated plants in South Wales – Port Talbot or Llanwern. This announcement came out of the blue, and steelworkers of South Wales were deeply shocked. The plants, two of five such works in the UK, were both modern, had both been blessed with substantial investment, and both had skilled workforces, the lifeblood of the Welsh people.

Soon after the announcement things began to be said and actions taken which alarmed me terribly. Some steelworkers of one plant began publicly denigrating the other and vice versa, and unless this was nipped in the bud the fine men and women of Port Talbot and Llanwern would be at each other's throats, declaring that it was not they who should be closed down but the other plant just a few miles away. I immediately called together our officials and representatives of the works to consider what we should do. Another strike was clearly not on. So we sat down and eventually came up with a plan which would involve the partial closure and streamlining of each of the two works. This plan envisaged some heavy redundancies on both sites, but I was convinced that if the base of each of the two works could be kept intact then, when better days came, we could see once again two flourishing works in South Wales. The representatives of each plant agreed and we then pressed the Corporation to adopt the plan, which we had carefully costed and presented to them in a constructive and professional way.

The Corporation, also weary from the thirteen-week dispute, accepted the strategy that we put before them. Once both plants had been saved we co-operated in driving down all manageable costs to as low a level as possible. This was a painful experience, but we knew it had to be done. It involved many workers giving up their own craft speciality and becoming steelworkers pure and simple – ready to do anything. It was rather like staff of a big company like BP agreeing to do anything that needed to be done – selling, cleaning, typing, drilling, driving or making the tea.

Today the two Welsh plants are hailed by government ministers, and acknowledged widely within the international steel community, to be two of the most efficient works in the world. None of this would have happened had not the steelworkers in South Wales co-operated to produce a well-argued document which the Corporation accepted. Another success, I am pleased to say, happened soon after Ian MacGregor became chairman of British Steel in 1981. This was the way in which we were able to save the Ravenscraig steelworks, as I shall later explain.

In a sense I was sorry to see Sir Charles Villiers go at the end of his contract period. For all his faults he did at least listen to another point of view, and he brought with him a burning desire to involve employee directors in the day-to-day work of the Corporation. Indeed, he increased their number and also brought representatives of the government and consumers onto the BSC board.

It was common knowledge that he and his chief executive, Bob Scholey, did not get on – something we had seen most clearly during the steel strike. I could tell that something was bound to break down in their relationship and was not really surprised when one day Bob Scholey called me and asked if he could see me privately. He told me that Sir Charles wanted to restructure the Corporation – to concentrate rather more decision-making power in his own office. Scholey said that Sir Charles was going to put the plan to a board meeting and he asked me if the employee directors on the board would support him and some others in trying to overturn the proposal. Scholey did not think the proposed changes would be good for the industry and doubted that Sir Charles really understood the steel industry.

I thought long and hard about what Bob Scholey had said and concluded that he was right. Whatever the differences we may have had in the past, this was clearly a time when we had to work together. I called together the employee directors and after some discussion it was agreed that we should oppose the structural changes proposed by Sir Charles (plans which had never been discussed with the trade unions), and the chairman's plan never saw the light of day. Looking back, I do not know whether we did the right thing. Sir Charles was certainly a million times better as chairman than the Scots-born American businessman we were about to endure.

Ian MacGregor came to us with a great reputation of being someone who gets things done. But all one can say about his tenure at British Steel is that he did not achieve a single thing that he set out to do. He declared to the world that he would bring British Steel back into profit. He failed. He declared that he would secure new exciting orders from around the world as Britain's super salesman. He failed. He said one of his priorities was to shut down the massive Ravenscraig steel plant in Scotland. And he failed.

Why he, being a Scot, wanted to do this, I do not know. There was no economic case for closing *any* of the big five integrated plants. But he was determined to shut one of them because one of his objectives, set by Margaret Thatcher, was to prepare British Steel for privatization. The government wanted to sell off all the profitable parts of

BSC and shut down the rest. It wanted to wash its hands of the steel industry, of that I am convinced. And Ian MacGregor knew that if any of the big five integrated works were to be sold to private investors then he had to sell it as a works which operated continually at over 90 per cent capacity, thus producing huge profits. The only way he could guarantee that these plants worked to this level was to shut one of them. Then customers for steel would be queuing up at the gates of the other four.

But which one could he shut? We had sacrificed to save the lives of both Port Talbot and Llanwern. So which was it to be – Teesside, Scunthorpe or Ravenscraig? Because of the three, Ravenscraig is the most distant from the steel-users, which are based largely in the Midlands and the South, and because transport costs are therefore that much higher, he picked on the Scottish works. Yet Ravenscraig has some of the most modern equipment and produces some of the finest steel in the UK, as many manufacturers and other customers will testify.

I knew what the horrific consequences of a Ravenscraig closure would be. It would pluck out the industrial heart of Scotland, and other Scottish steel plants would wither and die. Spin-off industries like engineering, transport and coal would collapse. When Ian MacGregor one day looked me in the eye and said, 'I tell you, Ravenscraig has got to go,' I knew we were in for a really hard fight.

First we prepared a paper setting out both the economic case for Ravenscraig's retention and the economic plight that would scar Scotland if the plant were to close. This was a well-argued case which drew compliments from the House of Commons Select Committee on Trade and Industry to which we submitted a great deal of evidence concerning the steel industry. Indeed, in all our dealings with the Select Committee we have won them over to our point of view on every single issue. Members of Parliament of all parties saw the logic of what we were saying, not only because it made sense, but because we presented it in a way they could readily appreciate.

We decided very quickly that if Ian MacGregor was to be

beaten, and if the Scottish steel industry was to be saved, then the only thing that would save it would be a *political* decision of the Cabinet not to let Ian MacGregor have his way. We therefore embarked on a substantial public relations programme involving all sectors of the community, and it was not long before all the major bodies in Scotland – local councils, community organizations, the CBI and even the Conservative Party – were at one with us in fighting to retain the most important industrial plant in the country. We spent a great deal of time with these organizations, persuading them that they ought to speak up for Scotland and put direct pressure on the government. In some instances we showed them how to do this. Our members in Ravenscraig itself did a brilliant job of involving every sector of Scottish life in our struggle.

We decided to hold in London a 'Steel Appeal Day', the focal point of which would be a rally in Westminster Central Hall, not just for trade unionists – that would cut no ice with the government at all – but for community groups, church leaders and councillors from areas around Ravenscraig and other steel plants. This was to take place on 23 November. We invited a whole range of speakers who would reflect what people felt about the need to maintain industry – we had church leaders, council leaders and political personalities from all parties, including Teddy Taylor, Conservative MP for Southend, who gave a blistering attack on the very notion that the Ravenscraig works ought to be closed.

We then lobbied Parliament and, more important, took a delegation down to meet five members of Mrs Thatcher's Cabinet and their advisers. I think the ministers thought that they were going to face across the table some angry trade unionists. What they found was council and community leaders of all shades of political persuasion. It is one thing for Mrs Thatcher to tell trade unionists to go away and not to bother her, but how could she say that to the Roman Catholic Archbishop of Scotland? Indeed, the Secretary of State for Scotland, George Younger, said that if the government allowed Mr MacGregor to have his way then he himself would resign from the Cabinet. This was an important breakthrough and was just the kind of political leverage we were looking for.

That, plus the enormous pressure exerted by the people of Scotland, together with the strong newspaper editorials which we had secured on behalf of our campaign and the support we received from the House of Commons Select Committee, forced the government to declare that the life of Ravenscraig was secure in the medium term. My colleagues are now working on the longer-term strategy to ensure that Ravenscraig continues to sustain the Scottish economy.

Ian MacGregor was absolutely furious that he had been rebuffed. 'But I tell you, I am not finished yet,' he told me angrily. He then hit upon what he thought was a magnificent idea. He would enter into an agreement with US Steel, the large American producer, whereby Ravenscraig would simply make liquid steel and then ship it in semi-finished form to the USA where it would be rolled by one of US Steel's plants. This would enable Mr MacGregor to shut down all the rolling mills in Ravenscraig and lay off half the workforce. His objective was crystal clear: once Ravenscraig was crippled it would not be long before he would be able to kill it off.

We were determined to beat this ploy too. I immediately contacted our colleagues in the American Metals Union, the United Steel Workers of America, and met them on the island of Jersey where we were holding our Annual Conference. They were as alarmed as we were about the plan because the American plant would also be crippled in that its steelmaking end would be shut and it would simply roll the material sent from Scotland. But what were we to do?

Here is yet another example of the kind of thinking that trade unionists today need to adopt. It would have been all very well to embark on more industrial action, but what would that achieve? We decided to have a joint advertising campaign in key journals likely to be read by decision makers here in Britain to point out the foolishness and economic madness of the MacGregor plan. We also made sure that the leaders of the American steel union gained prime time on television here in Britain to put their case against the plan. Mr MacGregor, I am sure, would have preferred us to have a strike. That is the kind of action he understands and that is the kind of action he can beat, as we have seen only too clearly in the coal dispute. But what he cannot fight is a skilful propaganda campaign – he runs away or resorts to putting plastic shopping bags over his head! We knew we had him on the run and it was not long before both U S Steel and Mr MacGregor announced that the plan was dead.

This made the sour Scot even angrier, and I am sure it came as a relief to him as well as to us when the government asked him to move on to tackle coal and Mr Scargill.

So now it was welcome to Bob Haslam, who would be part-time chairman, taking time off from his work at Tate and Lyle. When I met him I impressed upon him the need for as much consultation and participation as possible, and urged him to bring back to life the employee director scheme which Ian MacGregor had virtually stamped out during his short time with the industry. Bob Haslam seemed receptive, and there is every indication that he will handle his chairmanship with more imagination and care than his predecessor.

15

Triple Alliance:
The Terrible Trio

While we were battling with Ian MacGregor there was a
development about which I take some pride. I approached
Joe Gormley, the president of the National Union of
Mineworkers, and Sid Weighell, general secretary of the
National Union of Railwaymen, both friends of mine, with
a view to bringing back to life the old Triple Alliance of
unions in the coal, steel and rail industries. Between us we
represented Britain's three basic industries and what we
wanted was to become a new pressure group working on the
government for support of these basic industries in the form
of investment and modernization. We also wanted to give
each other as much help and co-operation as we could. We
in steel were committed to using British coal and to
transporting raw materials and finished goods by rail. The
mineworkers, for their part, were obliged to use British
steel in the mines and the railworkers were insistent upon
both British steel for rail track and equipment and British
coal for use within their industry.

The three of us shared the same political outlook – that of
Moderate Socialists who wished to see change within our
society brought about by natural evolution. Consequently
the hard left immediately dubbed us 'the terrible trio' and
began slinging their mud. But we did not have time to waste
in verbal fisticuffs: our job in 1981 was to meet with
ministers and persuade them that the fabric of Britain's
basic industry needed to be strengthened. Joe Gormley's
view was that coal, rail and steel and other heavy industry

were receiving little support from the TUC – a body seemingly now dedicated to the support of public services and the service industries. The TUC had become in effect a white-collar organization for white-collar workers and we felt that we had to take some initiative on our own. Certainly our meeting with ministers, especially Jim Prior, were cordial and we believe that we were instrumental in obtaining important funding for projects such as the electrification of sections of our rail network, further investment in mining and the introduction of more sophisticated plant at some of our steel works.

However, the character of the Triple Alliance began to change when Arthur Scargill took over from Joe and Jimmy Knapp took over from Sid Weighell. From the very beginning Arthur wanted to build into our objectives automatic strike action when one of us called upon the others to become involved. I could see immense dangers in this. If every time one of our unions withdrew its labour and called upon the others to take similar action then it seemed to me that we would all be for ever on strike! On the other hand I could see that there might be an occasion when the three of us ought to take action together, and I was willing to accept this eventuality. But I was still being pushed to the point where the original objectives of the Triple Alliance were to take second place to the new aggressive spirit that Arthur Scargill wished to promote.

I persuaded my colleagues to call a meeting of the executives of the Triple Alliance unions and there, in Congress House, I was able to persuade a wider audience that we ought to remain first and foremost a pressure group. We then embarked upon a series of rallies around the country, and at some of these meetings it was quite obvious that Mr Scargill had positioned his stormtroopers so that when it was my turn to speak I was met by booing and abuse.

We had expanded the Alliance to take in other unions in the three industries such as ASLEF, the Blastfurnacemen, NACODS and the Transport Salaried Staffs Association; this gave our grouping a more moderate stance and I had every hope that we could assert its true role. However, the extremists were out to have it their own way or nothing, and soon afterwards Mick McGahey labelled it the 'Cripple Alliance'.

Things began to disintegrate during the miners' dispute. We heard some left-wing critics declaring that the Triple Alliance should have given all-out support to the NUM, yet at no stage did Mr Scargill once ask for a meeting and, if he had, the majority of the seven unions would have told him that they were not prepared to wreck their own industries and that, in any case, he was running the strike in quite the wrong way.

It is fashionable at the moment to knock trade union leaders in the style of Joe Gormley and Sid Weighell – dedicated men who understood their people, believed in Britain, and wanted to do what was just and right – but I think it will not be too long before we look back and see that the approach that they had was right. Too often today trade union leaders want to sit on the fence and will not challenge what is being said even though they know it to be untrue.

One of the most difficult decisions I had to make was to challenge Mr Scargill's contention that the miners gave the steelworkers total support during our own strike. I felt constrained to produce documents to prove that steel moved from stock into the pits throughout our strike, that coal output during our dispute was the highest for seven years, that miners had more earnings during our strike than at any other time, and that within the coalfields support for steelworkers during their strike was rejected overwhelmingly time and again.

It is difficult to say publicly that a fellow trade union leader is not telling the truth, but truth matters, and if the Labour and trade union movement loses its grip upon that essential quality then we are going to lose the hearts and minds of the people of Britain.

16

The March of the Mods

While leading the national steel strike, I was trying to keep in touch with developments in the Labour Party. The Party was being wrested from its traditional moderate stance – change by evolution not revolution – by the hard left which had clustered round Tony Benn and assumed the name Bennites. I felt very strongly that in fact Tony – who was so understanding, receptive and helpful to us in our struggles with Monty Finniston – was being used by those who would like to see the Labour Party go down in flames so that they could resurrect a hard left party from the ashes.

I became involved with a group of moderate trade union leaders and MPs who were seeking to change the balance of the National Executive Committee of the Labour Party by supporting candidates who did not have extreme left views. They blamed the extremists for having been such a thorn in the flesh of Jim Callaghan, who as Prime Minister had had enough to cope with running a minority government.

The first two or three years of my involvement were out in the open on the platform at Labour Party conferences when I gave support to moderate MPs such as Shirley Williams, David Owen and William Rodgers and others. There were other trade union leaders on the same platform, including Tom Jackson, Alf Allen and Roy Grantham, but we were few and the impact we were having was very small.

In the mid-seventies the Hard Left, with its links with Militant Tendency, then took majority control of the Labour's NEC. We realized that if we were to defeat them, we had to learn some lessons and use some of their tactics.

I was involved in drawing together a group which was

trying to evolve a policy helpful to the Labour Party as a whole. Our early meetings took place in the Charing Cross Hotel, and included at different times Denis Healey, Frank Chapple, David Basnett, Terry Duffy and Roy Grantham. It was very difficult to get a measure of agreement between David Basnett of the General and Municipal Workers and Frank Chapple of the EEPTU. Frank, for his part, was so extreme in his right-wing views that at times even I would cringe at the statements he made! Although he withdrew from the group, Frank always ensured that his colleagues from the EEPTU were in attendance and gave full support. On the other hand David Basnett was a great disappointment. He stayed aloof and unco-operative. We could never persuade him of the need to join us in making sure that the Labour Party became once more the party of progress and moderation. He preferred sitting on the fence.

Terry Duffy on the other hand, president of the AUEW, who took over after the retirement of Hugh Scanlon, came out strongly for change. On Terry's introduction to the group he immediately gave us his full commitment; within three years, he felt, he should be able to line up the engineering union on the moderate wing of the Party.

When Jim Callaghan resigned as Leader of the Labour Party the first contender to throw his hat into the ring was Denis Healey. I was very pleased. Denis was just the man to take the Tories on and to put new heart into the Party; but he was not universally welcomed by all sections of what is a coalition of interests. A little later, Michael Foot, urged on by left-led unions like the Transport and General Workers Union, let his name go forward.

My union and I backed Denis Healey, who at that time was a target of every Militant Tendency 'rent-a-mob' determined to shut him up. Once the decision had been taken, however, and Michael Foot became our leader, I and my union gave him complete support. I had known Michael for a number of years and we always got on extremely well, but he was too kind and tolerant a man to guide the Party successfully back to power.

During the next year or so I and fellow moderate trade

union leaders continued to work as a group and on the odd occasion met in the St Ermin's Hotel near the Houses of Parliament. The press discovered that meetings had been held and for months afterwards talked vaguely about the 'St Ermin's Group', which I suppose is as good a title as any for those of us who were working together on what was a common cause – though purely in our individual capacities. I was rather amused when Peter Heathfield of the NUM sent me a letter in June 1984 (during our Annual Conference) addressed to 'Bill Sirs, c/o St Ermin's Hotel, Scarborough'!

Shirley Williams was always prominent at our meetings as a member of the NEC and described the difficulties the Party was having with the factions on the Executive. We began to get new members onto the Labour Party's NEC, Michael Foot seemed more determined to fight Militant Tendency and things became a little brighter, but after two years' work we still had not completely won the votes of the engineering workers.

During the third year of our activities there was a Special Labour Party Conference at Wembley Conference Centre in February 1981. For both the hard left and the mods this was the crunch. The hard left wanted to strengthen its position by having an electoral college elect the Leader of the Party instead of just the Labour MPs. I felt that this was ridiculous. The only people who know someone well are those who work with him day by day. Yet here was a suggestion that thousands of people who read only what the media write about the political superstars should become involved in the procedure. How can *they* tell if a man or woman is able, charitable, loving, efficient?

Shirley Williams had told me that she and David Owen and Bill Rodgers were contemplating leaving the Party; much depended on the Wembley Conference. As it happened, that Conference was a further setback. As the hard left forced one victory after another, Shirley Williams came up to me and asked to have a word. We stepped out into a corridor.

'We're going to go, Bill. I'm sorry, but we just can't stand it any more. We're going to create a new party – I'm terribly, terribly sorry.' She seemed apologetic and a little embarrassed. I think it was Roy Jenkins who, having ended his term as president of the EEC, played the key role in persuading the others to come out.

I was shocked by the news. We had been fighting together to save the soul of the Labour Party, not to abandon it. Yet I could understand Shirley's feelings. To me, she is a true Socialist – demanding change in society yet generous-hearted and loving. Beware those who philosophize and talk about the Socialist dawn yet treat the humble junior typist in their office with little short of contempt.

Back in the conference hall I talked to some of my colleagues. 'Shirley and the others are going,' I said. 'They've had enough.' We were sad and disappointed, and a little let down. Now, when I see Dr David Owen berating the trade unions I wonder what has happened to him. A pink Conservative now, he struggles to emerge as the leader of the Alliance. I worked with him a good deal over the years and not once, for instance, did he complain about trade union support of the Labour Party or union voting practices. Only now, when he has left us, does he find us so objectionable.

After the Wembley Conference we began to meet more regularly. Eventually our group of moderates succeeded in changing the balance of power on the NEC to give Michael Foot and his closest supporters the leeway they wanted. I remember meeting Shirley Williams later and reminded her of her charge that we would never succeed in making the changes necessary. 'Oh ye of little faith!' I chided her.

The willingness of top officials in a number of unions to give up their free time to discuss matters with prominent MPs and then to persuade their members what needed to be done resulted in a further strengthening of the moderate position on the NEC. Our task would have been much easier if only David Basnett had supported us fully. He dillied and dallied and sat on the fence and, although he privately condemned Militant Tendency and the hard left, he seemed unable to take an outright stand. There is absolutely no doubt in my mind that Militant Tendency was a party within the Party, with its own officials, paid staff and a newspaper. We succeeded in turning the tide against them but they are still there as a silent threat. Within five years, however, I anticipate that they will be put to flight.

Michael Foot's election campaign of 1983 was a disaster for Labour. Our manifesto promised the sun, the moon and the stars; certainly that is how the public saw it. We put the emphasis on nuclear disarmament (a sure vote-loser) and getting out of the EEC (in which the public was not the least interested); unemployment and the way in which our social services were being fragmented passed by almost unnoticed.

Somehow or other the Labour Party always seems to have the ability to frighten off ordinary workers. Somehow millions of ordinary people have gained the impression that the Labour Party is against the selling of council houses, yet that is not the case. The Party's position is that local councils ought to have a choice about whether they sell homes or not, as only *they* knew the situation locally.

So what went wrong? The Party's publicity machine was amateurish and Michael himself was portrayed as a kindly but exhausted man, a spent force. This was partly of the Party's own doing. I well recall Michael turning up at a meeting in South Wales to rapturous cheers but the look in his eyes told me that he hardly knew whether he was in Manchester, Middlesbrough or Merthyr Tydfil. The Party had rushed him around Britain, and he had spent days travelling and hours meeting handfuls of people, whereas he should have gone from TV studio to TV studio in a few of our major cities.

When, after the election Michael resigned, the left-led unions decided that Neil Kinnock should be their man. Indeed, I suspect that they had decided that some months before. Neil I knew to be very able and an attractive personality, and he had much to offer. He wants to see some fundamental changes in our society, but he knows we have to take the people of Britain with us.

I was determined that as the union was now to have some say as to who the next Labour leader should be then that decision ought to be made by as many people within the union as possible. We therefore asked all our 800 branches to let us know their views and the Executive Council invited all those who were contenders to come and speak to us. In the event Roy Hattersley and Peter Shore came to speak. I thought Roy Hattersley performed particularly well. Nevertheless, the Executive selected Neil Kinnock by thirteen votes to eight, partly I am sure because of his interest in and geographic involvement with steel. The press was naturally interested that a moderate union had picked Kinnock. Our decision tipped a number of other unions Neil's way.

It is fortunate that alongside Neil stands Roy Hattersley and the new general secretary of the Labour Party, Larry Whitty. I have great faith in Larry. He was once the secretary of the Trade Unions for Labour Victory Organization, and I came to know him as a very able man, young enough to have the ambition, imagination and incentive to do the job required of him – to pull together a party administration which can present to the public all that is good in Labour's philosophy. The Labour Party must become a campaigning party. Its headquarters in Walworth Road needs to be streamlined – something I know Larry will see to – and much greater resources given to the campaigning and publicity departments. Labour's Jobs and Industry Campaign, which is working towards the next general election, is the most promising sign I have seen that Labour is getting its act together. It is based upon carefully thought-out policies for different sectors of industry and is involving industrial communities in the discussion of how we should proceed. The campaign is also projecting excellent publicity material.

What ordinary steelworkers want, and I am sure the people of Britain want too, is a progressive government that will invest in British industries and in the skills and talents of the British people and do what it can for the whole community, not just for the most wealthy 5 per cent. That is the kind of party the Labour Party must be, and I have no doubt that Neil, Roy and Larry Whitty will encourage it to move swiftly in that direction. I am more optimistic about Labour now than I have been for many years.

Certainly we cannot tolerate the economics of the present government for much longer. It is only when they see British industry, abandoned by the government, being allowed to disintegrate, to the delight of our international competitors, that people will realize how serious the problem has become. One of the difficulties is that vast sections of the population never come face to face with the problems of industry and therefore do not know what we are enduring. Unless there are some changes, what they will come to know is the consequences of allowing our industries to die. They will awake with a shock when they find plummeting living standards, the disappearance of the welfare state and free education, and a jobless and uncaring society.

Neil Kinnock, as I am sure the British people will learn, has much to offer the nation. His constituency in Wales is close to the Llanwern steelworks and many of our members are his constituents; naturally we have come into contact over the years. Neil has been regarded as a man of the left or, now, the soft left. It is probably better to think of him as a progressive radical Socialist who is not afraid to accept challenges of either the right or the left and is tough enough to take on all opposition in the House of Commons. He is the sort of person who is quite capable of admitting mistakes if he should ever make them, because he has a degree of humility. He is also very good company.

I recall one Labour Party Conference when, after a 'Panorama' programme from Blackpool, I had dinner with some of the participants. Afterwards we joined Robin Day and his producer and other BBC representatives. Neil Kinnock was there, and for the next three hours we indulged in a singing contest in which we worked our way through every song known to us. I discovered that both Robin Day and Neil shared my taste in music. We formed a wonderful trio!

17

My Final 'Steel Appeal'

When I retired as general secretary of the ISTC on 6 January 1985 I looked back over the years in which the steel industry had shrunk dramatically, as indeed it had done in all advanced industrial nations. But private sector steel companies were now breaking even or making profits, and the British Steel Corporation itself would have made a profit in 1984–85 but for the coal dispute. That means our industry is back on keel and I was pleased to leave it, and my union, in good heart. We had also restored steelworkers to their rightful place at the top of the industrial pay league, as we have such a dirty and dangerous job, and our productivity at all plants could not be matched.

Two other events also gave me a great deal of satisfaction. First, we agreed with the National Union of Blastfurnacemen a merger proposal that their members join the Confederation, and this has now taken place. It unites all production workers in one union and hastens the day when there is a single union in the industry. This I still believe to be absolutely imperative.

Secondly, for years there had been arguments between ourselves and the Steel Industry Management Association about the recruitment of senior staff from those workers who are on the management borderline. This was resolved at the TUC when both parties signed an agreement with Norman Willis, the TUC general secretary.

One thing which still concerns me, however, is the government's long-term intention for steel. I am, as I said, sure that it wants to privatize the viable sections of the industry and shut down the unprofitable parts. This would be dogma gone mad, and would result in the wholesale collapse of steel. Already the industry has seen sections of plants hived off and sold to private interests, and the service has suffered in consequence. In the same way that hospital services have been privatized and patients are now having to suffer soiled sheets and dusty operating theatres, so in steel the main back-up services are beginning to deteriorate as they pass into the private sector, which is out to make a fast buck. Even worse, the workers in these private companies – often the very people who were doing the same job for British Steel – are being forced to accept lower pay, fewer holidays and no sickness or other benefits. Small private companies are not willing to pay properly – they have to force down pay to compete for contracts. If this is the way we are going as a society, then it will not be long before we get back to the days when unemployed men and women stood at factory gates waiting to be called in for a day's work. It will be back to the twenties and thirties with a vengeance.

Those who work in commercial companies, snug in their offices perhaps, may smile at the suggestion, but I can assure them that things are becoming extremely serious. There are millions of fellow citizens, and scores of communities that are suffering great hardship, and the total ignorance of this in certain areas of the country and especially in the South, astonishes me. It seems that there are now two Britains a world apart and one has no idea what the other is like.

My final 'Steel Appeal' would be for the government to withdraw its privatization proposals and allow the industry to continue to improve so that it can meet the needs of British manufacturing companies in the next decade. It can then give its workers a decent standard of living and make profits, part of which will be passed back to the Exchequer to be spent on schools, hospitals and social services. I would like to see the development of the employee director system; this will have to come if the European Commission has its way. I hope even at this late stage that some relief will be given in energy costs. Steel plants use such huge amounts of electricity that we should have a special tariff rate.

I hope that after Bob Haslam has finished his term as chairman, he is succeeded by someone who can unite the workforce so they can work together for success. And I hope that steel becomes a shining example to the rest of our industrial society.

18

The Future of Trade Unions

The Labour Party, as I said, faces rising fortunes and I only wish I could say the same thing about the trade union movement because there are certainly some changes which we still need to bring about in that body.

I regard the trade union movement as the most important and influential voluntary movement in the whole of the world. When we are acting constructively, as we ought to be within our national domain and on the international scene, the objectives have always been to improve standards of living and working conditions.

Unfortunately our weaknesses are quite considerable. As a movement we are structurally outdated and there are many examples in industry where an employer has to deal with a number of different trade unions in the same works.

Within the steel industry the British Steel Corporation had to deal with as many as seventeen different trade unions. This is unsatisfactory and extremely wasteful of everyone's time and resources. The unions involved differ in many respects. Quite often the rule books give different rights to members of separate unions. In some unions shop stewards take a positive role in making decisions. This was the policy adopted in the 1960s whereby the T & G and the AUEW leaders were saying the shopfloor was rule. One of the difficulties of this policy, which was adopted by Jack Jones, was that while the powers were being handed to the shop stewards, the responsibilities for their actions was not brought home to them with the same degree of authority. Power without responsibility can be very dangerous, whether in the hands of management or the trade union official. In some unions where shop stewards have taken decisions involving industrial action, the full time officials of that union have not been allowed to become immediately involved but have had to wait for the invitation of the branch or requests of their Executive Council.

Within my union, the ISTC, the disciplines and procedures are rather different. No shop steward or branch official is entitled to take any industrial action unless he requests and acquires the consent of the Executive Council. Naturally with attitudes as they are today we do sometimes have spontaneous stoppages on our hands, but the difference in our union, in such cases, is that our officials do have the right to involve themselves directly in the dispute with the objective of persuading members to go back to work so that procedures of negotiation can be followed. In order for the membership of a trade union to follow this procedure there has to be trust and loyalty to the union and its officers.

Another of the trade union movement's problems is the degree of political involvement and the support the union movement as a whole gives to the political arm of the movement. In the main the trade union movement is affiliated to the Labour Party but within the movement the unions are split almost down the middle in support of the extreme left or a moderate traditional Labour Party approach. One of the problems that faced Len Murray arose because time and again the TUC were split in their approach to dilemmas by political attitudes. The NGA's dispute with Eddy Shah is a good example of a difference in approach between unions of the left and unions of the right – the latter being for moderation and not breaking the law.

In addition many unions have different constitutions. The AUEW and other unions for instance have district committees which have powers of decision over industries within that district. This can sometimes place at a disadvantage an industry that does not have a single representative on this district committee. I recall the occasions in the North East when there was a dispute at the BSC South Works on the blastfurnace. The district committee of the Boilermakers took decisions that led to an escalation of the problem and yet not a single member of that district committee worked in the steel industry.

Another problem existing within the trade union movement involves the different methods of election. This has been widely publicized because of the Conservative Government's determination to force the trade union movement into a postal ballot system. Within the trade union movement officers are either elected or appointed. It is usual for the elected officers to have a vote within the Executive Council chamber. The appointed officers do not normally have a vote and their jobs are very little different to those managers in industry whose strength is that of merit and persuasion. In other words, they can be dismissed in the same way as any other worker, but if a person is *elected* to a position, unless he contravenes the constitution under which he is working dismissal would be a very difficult matter. Both systems have support within the trade union movement. Personally I prefer the method of appointment, the reason being that if a general secretary is appointed he must at all times obey the constitution of that union or risk dismissal by his employers, the Executive Council.

Those elected by the membership are conscious at all times of the need to keep a smooth relationship with his members who would vote him into his official position, and like a parliamentary election, when officers reach the period about a year prior to election they have to tread very carefully so as not to create electoral problems for themselves. This could mean that the decision-making is influenced by the forthcoming elections.

Three main systems of voting operate. There is the postal ballot, the pithead ballot and the branch ballot. None of these methods is completely foolproof, but the way to ensure that everyone gets the opportunity of a vote is to adopt the postal ballot. Unfortunately this does mean that unions have to have the names and current addresses of all of their members and pay for the sending out of the ballot envelopes and also return of those envelopes. With the installation of computer systems this is becoming easier but is still costly. Whilst the government has offered assistance towards postal ballot payments the trade union movement fears the price for this would be some form of interference and therefore there is a strong reaction against the widespread adoption of this system.

Secondly we have the pithead ballot. This is quite a good system and where it is monitored properly it is quite fair, but it usually applies to organizations that have a static membership or one that is contained within single departments or works as it operates by placing a ballot box or a number of ballot boxes at convenient places such as clock-in stations. At the same time independent observers are on hand to check that only one ballot paper at a time from each individual is placed in the box. In addition the observers at the end of the ballot ensure that the box is taken to a central position where votes can be checked and counted again by independent people.

The third method is the branch ballot system. My union used to operate this way and the accountants used to complain about the possibility of block voting, and that is why I replaced the branch ballot.

It is rather difficult for massive unions like the T & G to adopt the pithead type ballot because many of their members engaged in transport travel quite a lot and there would be difficulty in ensuring that they were present when the pithead ballot was held. The branch ballot means that everyone in the branch must be aware of the election that is taking place and the meetings being held to complete the branch ballot. This again can be extremely difficult and the way in which trade unions quite often have to overcome this problem is by taking space in newspapers, advertizing the fact that elections are being held and telling members what they must do, in the hope that all members see these advertisements. That is in addition to all the branch publicity that is going out.

I am not enamoured with the branch ballot system. My belief is that every member should have the opportunity of casting his vote and this therefore can only be done by a postal ballot. Ironically if the government had not been so anti-trade union and not been so insistent on the postal ballot system it is possible that most unions would have adopted this voluntarily. Governmental pressure paid off for no one.

It appears to me that in time, as trade unions do modernize, we will move to a system of postal ballots but this, of course, without government help, involves high costs that many trade unions cannot afford.

This brings us to the question of subscriptions paid by the members. There is no doubt that British workers get their trade unions on the cheap and at the TUC we have been looking at the way ahead relating to the contributions paid in general by trade unionists. We find that there is a large range of contributions charged by unions. In the main, however, the average British worker pays approximately half a per cent of his earnings per week. Many unions receive far less. The range of payments can be from 30p per week to around 80p per week. Some unions do charge more but this is unusual, and some unions spend the whole of their income on the membership's needs. There are certain unions that do not give service commensurate with the contribution income, but there are very few unions that are able to build up their funds on the low percentage subscriptions received within Britain.

If we compare this with our German, Swedish, American counterparts we would see that they normally would pay about two hours salary per month to the trade union. This would be over 1 per cent of their earnings and most of the unions in the countries mentioned above have massive contingency funds that can be used for the care of their members.

In looking at our overseas counterparts we also have to look at their structure as opposed to the British structure and here we have much to learn. In the main, the unions are organized in these countries on a broad *industrial* basis. For example, the huge German trade union, I G Metall has 2½ million members in all the metalworking business, steel, car manufacture, engineering, shipbuilding and so on. The employers in all of these industries have only one trade union hierarchy to deal with. They have only one trade union constitution to understand and respond to.

The German trade union movement is unique in that the British, through Ernie Bevin, shortly after the war, set up the structure of the trade union movement which now outdates the British structure. It was possible to recreate the German trade union structure on this industrial basis because Hitler had destroyed the original trade union movement. I certainly hope that we in this country will not be placed in a comparable position before we change our trade union structures.

The Americans, the Swedes, the Germans and Japanese all operate on the basis of total membership rights within whole industries or factories. If we are to return to the industrial stability that used to obtain in this country there has to be some rationalization of the union movement. This would considerably improve the industrial relations in the country. By the same token, of course, I would expect to see a change in management and government approach. In all of the countries mentioned, tripartite meetings and co-operation take place whether it be by industrial democracy or committee structure between government and management and trade unions. In Britain our links with the management are fragile and patchy, our links with the government non-existent. How can a country which must base its future on the ability to manufacture succeed whilst we have such a fragmented approach in each important sector of the economy.

When I look at the huge duplication of effort and cost in the trade union movement I am bound to confess that it is easy to establish the structures that will eliminate such problems – but only on paper. How can we manage our affairs in such a way that we would be able to put behind us the present ambitions and present prejudices? Far too often in the past we have seen the desire to increase membership purely to give block voting strength within the TUC or the Labour Party. Too often we are allowing the merging of unions across industries without ensuring that such mergers take place with the ultimate view of creating a single union in each of the major industries.

Mr Terry Duffy, President of the AUEW, and myself were convinced that given the time we might have been able, along with the EEPTU to create a single metalworking organization with all the separate strands necessary for the industries we would cover. To achieve such an ambition, however, would be extremely hard and naturally the TUC, who represent all unions, saw and see the problems as insuperable. But if the movement is to prosper efforts must be made in this direction. If one looks into the TUC archives dating from 1962–68 it can be seen that the secretariat under George Woodcock, then General Secretary, had proposed radical changes involving trade union mergers that would have considerably improved the efficiency and strength of the movement. It is unfortunate that all the constructive plans have not been implemented. It appears that general secretaries and presidents of unions are not prepared to surrender their power base in order to create a more efficient trade union movement.

I only hope that Mr Norman Willis the new General Secretary of the TUC will adopt a radical, constructive and even aggressive approach to union amalgamation. When I look at the numbers of journals and publicity papers produced by the trade union as a whole, including the TUC, it does seem that the movement could help hugely in the creation of a national newspaper that would support Labour. Whilst demands have been made before for this, under the present structure all efforts have failed.

Many of the unions have their own education facilities and duplication here again is costly. The TUC are very much involved in the educational field and yet at the same time many unions spend large amounts of money on their own educational needs. Much expensive duplication takes place, at a time when governmental education cuts are a national scandal. Furthermore the legal systems operated by most unions often double-up. This, too, indicates the possibilities that exist if we were to consider how we could centralize our systems.

We have also seen the emergence of workers setting up their own industries. There may be many examples of failure, but there are also some of successes. My own view is that unions should not be afraid to take out shares in companies in which their members work. This would certainly allow those workers to have a greater influence in the industry's decisions affecting members of the union who work there.

We will also need a movement to provide ourselves with better press and public relations. I long for the day when we see television commercials advertizing the benefits of union membership – and if we are to have these we need to increase our income and that means putting up members' subscriptions.

I think we have to be a lot more imaginative too. Somehow we must capture the good will of the British people all over again. To achieve this we must do three things. We have first to reach the new generation of young people who know nothing about trade unions and explain to them exactly what we are about. This means television commercials, films, videos, comics and special booklets as well as promotion in schools. Secondly we have to let the public see the better side of trade unionism – all the millions of man hours of voluntary work that trade unionists do up and down the country, week in week out. The way in which we care for our sick and elderly workers, our pensioners; the way in which we support communities, welfare centres, social clubs, and all kinds of facilities for young people; the way in which we help to run our town councils, sit on the bench of the nation's magistrates' courts, and play a part in the cultural, artistic and religious life of our nation.

The vast majority of trade unionists, like the rest of the British people, are hardworking, loyal and patriotic. Yet this is not the image that the public has of a trade unionist. They see only the bawling, yelling, sloganizing ranter, the work-shy, idle, card-playing shopfloor worker or striker. These false images have to be removed before it is too late, and we must use every technique in the book to bring about a change in the public's perception of who we are and what we do.

Thirdly we need as trade unions to take up a still greater

share of life around us, entering all kinds of forums. For instance my own union heard of the plight of Britain's champion fencer, 22-year-old Bill Gosbee, who had hardly enough money to get to the Olympic Games and was crucially short of equipment. We stepped in to ensure that he got to Los Angeles in fine shape and with all that he required.

We are now sponsoring him until the next Olympic Games so that he is free of worries about income, and can spend all his time practising and concentrating on his sport. In turn, Bill, wherever he is in the world, praises the British steel foils that he uses, made from the finest steel in South Yorkshire. Most of the sports correspondents of our national newspapers in Fleet Street praised this sponsorship, the first of its kind, and it got wide publicity.

This is the kind of thing that more unions ought to be doing. I look forward to the day when the trade union movement sponsors the whole of Britain's Olympic squad, sponsors national football or rugby squads, supports National Eisteddfods, galas and opera.

There was a time when trade unionists – ten million of them – comprised the most powerful block in Britain because of their muscle. I want to see the day when Britain's trade unionists are more influential than ever before, not because of the power they can employ but because of the contribution they make to the life of the nation.

Before we can do this, perhaps we have to take some action to put our own house in order, which means that we must be seen to be absolutely and completely democratic and be recognized as a movement where the spirit of brotherhood and sisterhood is once again paramount.

My last act as general secretary of my union was to put into operation a campaign to win a 'yes' vote from our membership on the question as to whether or not we should continue to have a political fund out of which we could pay for political activity. It seems to me that the government's objective of denying trade unions not just the choice of affiliating to the political party of its choice but the right to have a voice in Parliament through sponsored MPs and to campaign for their industries, was utterly wrong.

I know only too well, especially during our campaign to keep Ravenscraig alive, how much political spadework has to be done to win the kind of result one seeks. If the government are to deny us access to the tools of democracy then unions have only one place to go – back to the days of industrial strife.

It seems that the role of trade unions is to persuade, and to influence public opinion, and thus to influence the decision-making process of our country. The Unions should not be robbed of that opportunity. Whether or not trade unions can take up the challenge facing them remains to be seen. But old ideas and old attitudes must give way to new thinking and new initiatives and for that we need new blood and new life.

Ten years' hard labour it has certainly been. Crisis after crisis, problem after problem. Trouble in steel, trouble in the movement, and trouble in the Party.

But I wouldn't have changed any of it. I love to run – but not to run away from problems. Despite all, as I go around Britain I see afresh what a wonderful country this is. We have so much talent, so much verve, so much love and consideration, what a shame it is that our structures, be they political, trade union or constitutional, so often let us down. If the country, managements, our trade unions and the Labour Party to which I am wedded can shake off yesterday and grasp tomorrow with both hands, I believe the really good times are still to come.

Index